LAMENT FOR RASTAFARI
and other plays

By the same author

UNDERGROUND – 4 plays
   The Wonderful Year (La Gente – The Workers)
   The Burghers of Calais (The Scottsboro Boys)
   Fun in Lethe
   The Mummer's Play
CRUCIFICADO
   Life and Times of J. Walter
      Smintheus

Children's books
THE CHILDREN OF NIGHT
SATI, THE RASTAFARIAN
OMAR AT CHRISTMAS

This book has been published with financial assistance from the Arts Council of Great Britain

LAMENT FOR RASTAFARI
and other plays

EDGAR WHITE

Marion Boyars
London . New York

Published in Great Britain and the United States in 1983 by MARION
BOYARS Ltd.
18 Brewer Street, London W1R 4AS and
MARION BOYARS Inc.
457 Broome Street, New York, NY 10013
Distributed in the United States by The Scribner Book Companies, Inc.

Australian and New Zealand distribution by Thomas C. Lothian Pty.
4-12 Tattersalls Lane, Melbourne, Victoria 3000

© Edgar White 1983

Library of Congress Cataloging in Publication Data

White, Edgar, 1947–
     Lament for Rastafari; and, Like them that dream.

     1. Blacks – Drama.   2. Race relations – Drama.
I. White, Edgar, 1947–   . Like them that dream. 1982.
II. Title.
PR 6073.H4918A6 1982   822'.914   91–69653
ISBN 0–7145–2763–X (cloth)
ISBN 0–7145–2756–4 (pbk.)

British Library Cataloguing in Publication Data

White, Edgar
Lament for Rastafari; and, Like them that dream.
I. Title
812'.54   PS3573.H46

Printed and bound in Great Britain by Biddles Ltd, Guildford and King's Lynn

CONTENTS

**For my children
Nicole and Harmakhus**

LAMENT FOR RASTAFARI

Lament for Rastafari deals with the journey, both spiritual and physical, of a West Indian family from Commonwealth to England and finally America

CHARACTERS

LINDSAY . . . A writer

BARRETT . . . A sufferer

LA PUTA (LILLY) . . . Illegitimate sister of Barrett

GOGITA . . . His legitimate sister

UNCLE PETER
FATHER . . . Aspects of the father

CHARLES WOLFE . . . Spiritual father to Lindsay

MOTHER
AUNT ETHEL . . . Aspects of the mother
HILDA

STANDFORD
MR SYMTH . . . The West-Indian middle class
MRS SYMTH

CELESTINA
RUDE BOY . . . The West-Indian survivors

The play can be performed with eight actors.

LAMENT FOR RASTAFARI

First production – April 1975, New York Shakespeare Festival
Public Theater. Directed by Basil Wallace.
CAST

Lindsay	Lou Ferguson
Barret	Sam Singleton
La Puta	Deirdre Lambert
Gogita	Arlene Quijoax
Mother	Rosana Carter
Father	Jim Liburd
Clayton	Duane Oliver
Minister	Roso Illis

Original music by Walli Obara

First London produciton – 1978, Keskidee Productions. Directed by
Rufus Collins.
CAST

Lindsay	David Haynes
Barret	Witty Forde
La Puta	Yvonne Giddins
Clayton and Father	T. Bone Wilson
Sandford	Imruh Caesar

Original music by *The Ras Messengers*

Second London production – 1981, Lumumba Productions.
Directed by David Haynes
CAST

Lindsay	Clifton Goldson
Barret	Everall Hall
La Puta	Eunice Allen
Father and Minister	David Whyte
Sandford	Gladstone Philips
Original music by *The Ras Messengers*	Yvonne Williams
	Sandra Edwards

ACT 1
JAMAICA

SCENE I

*The actors enter from throughout the theatre selling their wares in
the market place. Lady falls out and is brought round by the voodoo
of the old one. The crowd continues the ritual of early morning
bartering.*

Darkness.

SCENE II
STUDY OF WEST-INDIAN CRUELTY

Two soldiers and slave

SOLDIER I   Bring that boy here. I say bring that here.

SLAVE   You rass!

SOLDIER II   Strike him. *(They hit him)* Strike him. Cut his skin
hard. Cut him draw blood, draw blood. Can't you hit him
harder than that? Look he bleeding now. His blood good
on his skin. *(The soldier becomes ecstatic)*

Darkness

STUDY FOR PRISONERS

*It is mid-day. The prisoners are visible in their short khaki pants and
shirts open showing their sweating black skin. The impression is one
of pressure in on you. The audience must feel as if they themselves
were walking through a prison. The barbed-wire fence must be felt.
Scenes of lashings in background. The guards look like dressed up*

children since their pants are too short.
The location is the Guncourt, in Jamaica.

PRISONER I   *(Screaming as he walks)* Jah! Jah! Jah!

PRISONER II   Tell him, tell them for me, tell them King Alfa is a
prisoner in Guncourt. Tell them that the Lion of Juda is a
prisoner at Spanish Town.

PRISONER I   Tell them they lock up the Ras at general
penitentiary.

PRISONER II   Tell them if you don't have money then Jamaica is
a prison.

Their screams build to a wild chant

SCENE III
THE LANDLORD

Kumina is in her early twenties. Her face is prematurely serious. Her
head is usually wrapped with a bright red or white cloth. Depending
on the angle which you view her she appears to be very country-
looking or very African. She has a little boy named Raymond, he is
about five. She looks from the window and sees Mr. Samuels, the
Landlord, approaching. The time is early evening. Mr Samuels is
about forty, he looks well-fed and is always sweating.

KUMINA   Raymond go inside boy. Go on play inside. *(Boy says*
something to her) Oh Lord, look my cross here. Did you
hear what I tell you boy. Why you so hard-a-ears? Go on
inside that room, and turn off the radio, I don't want him
know we have a radio. *(Sound of footsteps and then*
knocking)

MR SAMUELS   Kumina, you in there?

KUMINA   *(Fixing herself, making sure the housecoat she is*
wearing is fastened) Coming just now. *(Opens the door)*
Oh hello, Mr Samuels.

MR SAMUELS   I knew you was home, I could smell the food, what you cooking?

KUMINA   Just cooking up soup.

MR SAMUELS   Lizard stew eh? *(He laughs and opens up his rent book)* Now you know you way behind on the rent, Kumina.

KUMINA   Yes, I know, but I . . .

MR SAMUELS   Now you know I don't like to have to chase people down on Sunday evening for they rent. *(Pause, sniffs for a minute)* You baking?

KUMINA   Just some bakes.

MR SAMUELS   Now what I must do with you girl, you know I been very patient with you. With all of you. But I losing more money than the damn thing worth. Look at all these names here in this book. All of these people owe me.

KUMINA   *(Looking over his shoulder)* I can't read too good but your money coming you know Mr. Samuels soon as I . . .

MR SAMUELS   I hear your man lock up in Spanish Town.

KUMINA   Who tell you so?

MR SAMUELS   Well so me yerrie, as they does say.

KUMINA   Look I'm going do some day work next week if you just give me until the end of the month, I have it for you.

MR SAMUELS   *(Like a father)* Kumina, what I must do with you. You not even going offer me no oxtail stew. *(He takes hold of the hem of her housecoat, she moves away from him)* All right then Kumina, you don't want to be nice to me but I must be nice to you, right? Listen I coming next week and you better look like you have something to give me. One way or the other you going give something up, or you and you pickney go right in the street, you hear me?

KUMINA   Yes, Mr Samuels.

> *Sounds of footsteps descending stairs and then he turns and knocks at another door*

MR SAMUELS   Gilvie, I know you in there, Gilvie. I could hear you radio you know. What you intend to do about this rent? You make me have to shame you before all these people. Well what you make up your mind for do?

> *Two youths come up behind him, all that is visible are red caps pulled down over their ears.*

MR SAMUELS   What you want?

> *Two gunshots sound*

KUMINA   *(From window)* Oh God.

VOICE OF MAN   *(From window)* Shoot him in him bloodseed.

> *The two young men vanish. The crowd immediately gathers as they exit. They enclose his body like a flock of ravenous birds. Silence follows, they too vanish taking the body with them leaving only Kumina on stage. She turns to the sound of little Raymond approaching.*

KUMINA   *(As in a dream)* Go inside Raymond, this not for you.

> *Slow Darkness*

SCENE IV
ODE TO CHARLES WOLFE

The entrance is night, caribbean and solitary. The sounds of the barking dogs is faint from the city below. Spirits walking duppy as they are called.

Lindsay has just been released from prison. There is the sound of burra drumming. This is the music which is played upon the release of a prisoner in old Jamaica.

We are in the mountains long and dark. We can see the kerosene lamps flickering in the yards of the few distant houses. You walk along an uncertain darkness and finally come upon a stand on the side of a road. Before the outline of a lamp you see a bearded man. He has a pot of food always on the stove and he awaits you. A man possibly in his fifties possibly older, back straight and eyes outward to the world.

LINDSAY   Good night to you sir, and God in this house.

CHARLES WOLFE   Love sir, you does favour a St. Thomas man. You people them from St. Thomas?

LINDSAY   No sir, my people them from far.

CHARLES WOLFE   *(Opening a large pot and stirring it with a ladle)* Here man, come eat. You look like you could stand it.

LINDSAY   *(Opening his hand to receive the food)* Love. The dread is on me, I feel a way.

CHARLES WOLFE   I'm a man as doesn't travel far. I build my stand here and I wait. Eventually all must pass here. And if they come by night they weary and if they come by day they weary.

LINDSAY   Food taste good man.

CHARLES WOLFE   You going go far?

LINDSAY   Yes, is far I going yes.

CHARLES WOLFE   Well, you must take some breadfruit and mango. These coconuts here you see nice. And you must go with this sugar cane.

LINDSAY   The sugar cane?

CHARLES WOLFE   Your history here boy.

LINDSAY   How you mean?

CHARLES WOLFE   This here man *(holding up sugar cane)* for this here you was put in bondage. For this same sugar cane. For this they bring you Jamaica. First there was JA, then there was MA, and finally JA- MA- CA. When them does refine this them make sugar.

LINDSAY   Yes, the sugar.

CHARLES WOLFE   And when them make the sugar, then them make the rum. The white rum. Now when you're weary from the day labour and the world come hard on you, you climbing the road and your rage come down on you because you see you is only a black beast.

LINDSAY   Yes.

CHARLES WOLFE   When your rage come on you then you bite down on the sugar cane. You suck it hard to bite back you rage and the juice come sweet on you. Then you must drink your white rum which came from the sugar cane. You going drink yes, because if you no drink then you want to kill a man because as I say, the rage on you.

LINDSAY   I must drink yes.

CHARLES WOLFE   Then when you drink you want bust you water with the daughters. *(Lindsay laughs)* Yes for true. You going want to roll on she belly like ripe guava berry. You can't help it. Is the white rum. She bumbo come up sweet to you like mango. And when you come inside she you jump like a let go beast. When you come inside she you must make a man child. Is why God put you here. You must make baby. I don't care how much book you read, you can't help make baby when the sun and the rum come on you.

LINDSAY   For a truth, yes.

CHARLES WOLFE   I know, I meself make 7 manchild and 5 daughters. But it all does come from this same sugar cane.

LINDSAY   But tell me now, why God make us so. Must we work like beast forever?

CHARLES WOLFE   Well see now, from the time of Adam, the first
black man, unto Jesus which was the second coming of the
black man, God put a curse on us for our blindness. And
God say, all I will give you to ease the pain of your bondage
is the ganja, the rum and the daughters. Is a kind of pain
they put on us. You know a kind of way? *(Pause)*. And it
make our music sweet. *(He stands and calls out to the
wind)*

SHANGO LOVE POEM
Shango, you know my woman
She's the other one
The dark one
And you see her last.

Shango, find my woman and touch her
Close for me.

Maybe you'll find her
In the morning
When the women walk from the hills
To the city
Their children following behind them
Making shadows following shadows.

You know my woman?
Her hands are a washboard
But her back is straight
Her daughter is five years old
She was born with gonorrhea
You know my woman
Maybe you'll find her in the morning
Or maybe you'll find she in the afternoon
Scrubbing the mulatto's floor
Go to her
Go on the trade winds of the afternoon
The same winds which brought
Columbus and our dread

Go on the tradewinds Shango
Cool her.
Maybe you'll find her at night, Shango
When the mad dogs scream out their history
Locked in their yards.

Find my woman, touch her close
Tell her that I am I
And one heart

You know my woman, Shango
She's the other one
The dark one the one you see last . . .

LINDSAY   Sometimes, you know, tears does come down on me. I feel it hard on me sometimes you know, but they does say that a man shouldn't cry.

CHARLES WOLFE   *(Sucking his teeth)* Cho. If beast does weep and trees does weep why not man, everything in God world cry. So then we no must.

LINDSAY   Yes.

CHARLES WOLFE   Listen, if you going down to Babylon, ask after a man there I does know. They call him Sugar Belly and him play sweet tune on bamboo fife. If you see him tell him, deep love and one heart.

LINDSAY   Airey. *(Somewhere in his eyes appear something very much like tears.)*

Darkness.

WASH DAY

Mother and daughter

MOTHER   You have the clothes ready, Kumina?

DAUGHTER   Yes, Mumma.

MOTHER   Well is what you waiting for. Kneel down and pound
them no.

DAUGHTER   *(Kneeling and pounding the clothes on a rock)* Yes,
Mumma.

MOTHER   So wha' happen', you no have no strength in you arm?
Juk the clothes no man. You too damn lazy. You burning
the candle at both ends. You don't know how for sleep
when night come right?

DAUGHTER   But what you want, you don't see me pound
the clothes.

MOTHER   Don't give me no back chat, girl. You can do better
than that. What that is there. A rust stain? Where's you lime
and salt? You go have for let that bleach with you second
wash and you must be careful with you starching. Last time
you left them shirt to come stiff like board.
You must be feel all a man want is a woman for cock up
she leg when night come. When you belly swell if you can't
keep a house he go dash you way, you watch.

DAUGHTER   Yes, Mumma.

MOTHER   Me say for juk the thing no man.

Darkness

SCENE V
ASPECTS OF THE VILLAGE

Presentation of wife to Mother

SON   *(Leading dark-skinned girl by the hand)* Mother I brought
someone I want you to meet.

MOTHER   Oh yes.

SON   This is Claudine, the girl I'm going to marry.

MOTHER   Oh Lord.

SON   What's the matter?

MOTHER   Why she so dark? You shouldn't marry a girl look so black. Why she fan she leg so, she hot?

Actors improvise to end of scene.

SCENE VI
MOTHER & DAUGHTER

DAUGHTER   Why you going to take my child from me?

MOTHER   What you know about child, you child yourself.

DAUGHTER   But you can't take him from me.

MOTHER   Girl have some sense, I know what best for you. I going to see to it that you never run the street again. Whenever you go out of this house again I going to spit on the ground and before that spit dry, I want to see you rass here, you hear me. When you can take care of responsibility, you is a woman. Until then you still a child all right.

Darkness.

GOSSIPING WOMEN

GIRL I   Hold still so I can plait your hair.

GIRL II   Lord Jesus don't pull so hard.

GIRL I   You tender-headed.

GIRL II   You hear Doris make a baby?

GIRL I   I did hear so yes.

GIRL II   Her mother take it.

GIRL I Who the father is?

GIRL II *(Bends and whispers his name)* Lindsay!

GIRL I Him again? He busy.

GIRL II So they say papa, me don't know for sure.

GIRL I Must be him yes. Well is over for her now. She stupid she must be going leave soon.

GIRL II Most naturally.

GIRL I Well me never like her, she too damn show off.

GIRL II But Sandra, didn't you make a baby?

GIRL I Turn your head, you're too damn fast.

　　Darkness.

SCENE VII
THE LADY AND THE SERVANT GIRL

It is morning in Kingston. The lady is addressing her servant girl who has just arrived by bus from the bush. The lady is, of course, light-skinned and petite. The servant girl is dark and strong and silent.

LADY Well Lilly, how are we this morning?

LILLY Feel very fit thank you, Mistress Smyth.

LADY You can take Cynthia for her stroll in the pram at eleven.

LILLY Yes, Mistress Smyth.

LADY And be careful now that you don't walk her in the sun. Her skin is very sensitive.

LILLY Yes, Mam.

LADY The dirty clothes are in foyer. You'll find the wash tub down stairs around the back. Be mindful of the dog.

LILLY   Yes, Mistress Smyth.

LADY   Now about dinner. My husband is very fond of ackee.

LILLY   Oh yes, ackee and salt fish Mam.

LADY   Yes, well pop down to the fish shop and get some when you go out at eleven.

LILLY   Ackee no come from fish shop Mam. Ackee plant.

LADY   Oh . . . really. Well wherever it comes from Lilly, pick some up.

LILLY   Yes, Mistress Smyth.

Lady exits

Lilly picking up large bag of laundry, talks to herself.

LILLY   Yes, Mistress lady, Lilly going walk you baby. Lilly going scrub you dirty drawers. Is Lilly going fix you food. But one day it not going be so. You going call Lilly and Lilly be long time gone. To rass. *(Pause)* Still I rather wok for coloured people than white. But I can't stand these backra people. They like for pose too bad.

She lights a cigarette and carries off laundry.

SCENE VIII
STUDY FOR ANGLICAN CHURCH

As the scene opens the priest, Father Peters, is being helped into his jacket by his wife Carol. She looks at him her eyes full of pride.

CAROL   I remember the first time I saw you in your collar. You look so well. I say he's a Minister, yes. *(She brushes the jacket)*

FATHER PETERS   You not sorry the Archdioceses sent me here?

CAROL   Any place you are is where I belong isn't it?

FATHER PETERS   But this is an exceptionally dull island I'm
            afraid. The people here are always testing you, just like the
            island, the hurricanes and cyclones.

CAROL   If you had married that white girl you were going to, they
            would have let you remain in England.

FATHER PETERS   *(After two beat pause)* I'm not sorry I didn't
            marry her, Carol.

CAROL   *(Already starting to leave)* I'm going to get the wash.

FATHER PETERS   People are always testing you. I remember that
            Feast of Epiphany in the January of the year. And that boy
            he couldn't have been but sixteen. He asked me if I
            believed this world could ever be any different for a black
            man? Different how I asked? Different so that a black man
            wouldn't have to be servant for any white man. I said, 'Yes,
            of course there will be a time when all men shall walk freely
            with no man having dominion over another.' But the words
            came too easily to me. A time, perhaps an eternity of
            silences away, when a black man can go anywhere or do
            anything in this world he chooses without dread. Then he
            asked me if I believed there was such a thing as a black
            spirit which has allowed us to survive the white man's
            cruelty. I said that I believed in a common bond, I didn't
            know if there was such a thing as a black spirit exactly. 'Well
            then, what is it you believe in?' he asked. 'I believe in one
            God, the Father almighty, maker of heaven and earth.'
            'And what, he asked of the things visible and invisible?' 'I
            believe in them both equally for God is surely invisible, yet I
            believe in Him.'
            'But *you* are God,' he answered. 'And you can't see
            yourself. Why are you like all West Indians? Why can't you
            believe? Why a *white* Jesus?'
            And my mind failed me then, and I could not answer him.

CAROL   Lord help this man, he's so lost.

SCENE IX
STUDY FOR BLACK BOURGEOISIE

The Spastic Ball

It is night. There is a basketball game at the Spastic Hospital. The black middle class are present because it is rumoured that the Prime Minister himself will attend. There are several stiff-looking light-skinned couples present. Notably, the Smyths of Manchester. Mr Smyth is a building contractor.

MR SMYTH   What the hell are we doing here? I should be home in my bed sleeping. I'm tired.

MRS SMYTH   Well everyone is here, dear. There are the Hills over there and the Stevens and the Whites. Look, even the Mays!

MR SMYTH   *(Irritated)* What the hell do I need to see them for when I have to deal with them all day?

MRS SMYTH   Look there, the Hills are waving.

MR SMYTH   *(Smiling)* Hi there, Hill. *(He waves mechanically)*

A round pompous black man takes the microphone as Master of Ceremonies

SPEAKER   Greetings to you ladies and gentlemen. I would like to welcome you to our Paraplegic Basketball Games. Unfortunately, this year, Prime Minister Seaga will be unable to attend due to more pressing matters of State.

MR SMYTH   *(to his wife)* See, I told you, Seaga ain't coming again.

SPEAKER   He has, however, sent his representative from whom you shall hear directly. As you may or may not know, there are over 10,000 registered spastics on the island. The hospital, is however, the largest of its kind and we specialize mostly in young people. And here, without further ado, are our players.

*Several spastics enter in wheelchairs. Some crawl across the
stage on their hands. Several of the girls have unusually
large breasts. Mr Hill, a tall, light-skinned East Indian from
an import and export company, comes over and speaks
with Mr and Mrs Smyth.*

MR HILL   My God, I see everyone's here. How are you, Margaret?
Edmund?

MRS SMYTH   Fine, and you?

MR SMYTH   Suffering. Could be worse, I guess.

MR HILL   You never get a Jamaican to say he's doing well. He's
always suffering. *(They laugh)*
(Bending over to whisper in Smyth's ear) Spent fifty
dollars for tickets to see this game. Must contribute to
charity etc. etc. Did you get a look at that centre girl's titties.
(Smyth now examines) She's looking quite fit, even though
the rest of her is paralysed.

MR SMYTH   Tell me, do you think they still have sex?

MR HILL   I should imagine. *(Becomes very medical for a
moment)* I can't see why one thing should impair another. I
mean below the waist they are still women. As far as I can
imagine they should be able to . . .

*Enter Piccong, a dark, weary looking man in a white
uniform. He is an ambulance driver.*

PICCONG   Begging your pardon, Mr Smyth, Sir.

MR SMYTH   Why Piccong, how are you doing fellow? You're
looking hale. Working for the hospital I see.

PICCONG   Yes, sir. You see my daughter's a patient here.

MR SMYTH   Really?

PICCONG   Yes, so you see when I couldn't get any more work
with your contracting firm, I kind of had to take this job.

MR SMYTH   You're a good worker, Piccong. I always like you.
The problem is that you only specialize in masonry.

PICCONG   Yes, sir, well since I've been here I've learned to drive
a truck real good, sir. But the pay here is hard, sir. I can't
take care of seven children on $22.50 a week. So I kind of
wonder if you have any part-time thing you want me to do
for you. It wouldn't get in the way of the ambulance
business.

MR SMYTH   *(Like the prince of a monarchy)* Come by tomorrow,
Piccong. We'll see what we can do.

PICCONG   Thank you, sir, thank you.

Smiling he steps backward and exits.

MR SMYTH   *(To Hill)* That's the problem with the poor people
here. They can only do one thing if they can do that.
(They turn to watch the game a second.)
(To Mrs Smyth) You know sometimes I wonder if they are
our prisoners or we are theirs.

*The action freezes. We see the spastics begin to encircle the
Smyths.*

Darkness.

SCENE X
STUDY FOR BUSH

*Lilly returns home after working all day for the Richards. She finds
her husband Lindsay and his friend Bo, sitting drinking white rum
and drawing ganja from a chalice. She enters, sees them, and says
nothing at first. She begins to straighten the house.*

LINDSAY   *(Looking up after exhaling a large cloud of smoke)* Is
now you fe come?

LILLY   Is waiting, I waiting for the damn bus on Hope Road for
must be two hours.

BARRETT   Hello, Lilly.

LILLY   How you doing, Bo?

BARRETT   Suffering as a man must.

LILLY   Him draw him ganja and drink him white rum and him suffering. *(Sucks her teeth)* Cho!

LINDSAY   What you fe cook, woman?

LILLY   We still have fry fish here. You no have wait upon me to come fix you food no.

LINDSAY   Listen woman, you must be want me thump you down this night. Is not fe me to cook. You is my woman is you must be here.

LILLY   *(Goes in the other room and starts dressing for the night world)* Man, you no easy you know.

LINDSAY   Where you for now?

LILLY   You know where I gone.

LINDSAY   *(Standing up now and grabbing hold of her)* I don't want you sell yourself to no more man.

LILLY   Oh man, please, don't start now. What me fe do. I going need money send for me mother. I swear to her that I going take her from the bush.

LINDSAY   You going take her from bush and what. This, this no bush? Where you going bring her? You must be have some mansion you going put she in.

LILLY   Look Lindsay, I promise her that, and I not going fail. Before she dead I going send for she. Cause I don't want she say: 'God cuss upon you', and if I must work all day and whore at night then so it must go. I gone.

LINDSAY   *(Looking at Bo and trying to save face)* Come back woman.

   (She exits) What the bumbo cloth you think this is? You is

me woman. Leave you mother in bush to rass.

BARRETT   *(Holding him)* Come on man, lick you pipe.

LINDSAY   Rass hole cloth. I going strike she dead this same night.
Watch me good.

BARRETT   Man, don't trouble up yourself. Lick you pipe, man.
Let she go. Let the daughter do what she must do, man.
Come on lick your pipe.

Use of simultaneous time while Bo is speaking with
Lindsay. On stage right, we see Lilly and stage left, the
Smyth family who she worked for that day.

BARRETT   With a woman you must only let them go on and do
them business in Babylon. For a woman will always survive
better than a man. As long as she got some flesh upon her
she make out better. So lick up pipe man . . .

They freeze. Lights come up on The Smyths. Mrs Smyth to
Mr Smyth – she is wearing the sort of soft mini shirt in
which the middle-class women usually greet their husbands
after a day of boredom and leisure.

MRS SMYTH   Edmund I wish you didn't have to go out tonight.

MR SMYTH   Yes, I know me love, but I must. *(She rubs his*
stomach with her hands)

MRS SMYTH   Do you really have to? I hardly see you. I've been
home all day taking care of your daughter. *(He reaches his*
hand up her dress and pats her softly on her bottom)

We turn again to Lindsay and Barrett.

BARRETT   *(To Lindsay)* If a woman walk the road and she just
leave one man you never know. If she just leave five man
you never know, cause all you does see is she alone and
you does desire her. Was always so, and will always be so.
That's why I say a daughter going survive better than a man
always. So lick up you pipe man and don't trouble up
yourself.

He is seated beside Lindsay. A large bottle of rum between
them.

BARRETT   But you know a nigger man is a sad thing in truth.

LINDSAY   The Lord is my shepherd I shall not want.

BARRETT   Is good that you don't want, cause you not going to
get in this man's world.

LINDSAY   Do you see the contented look on these contented
people?

BARRETT   Me never see a country before where even the
cows hungry. But me going go away from here.

LINDSAY   Not before me you not going.

BARRETT   Sometimes I sit and I think hard, hard on one thing.

LINDSAY   Money!

BARRETT   You damn right, money. Sometimes me think so hard
me head hurt me. But the harder me does scheme, it seem
it run further from me.

LINDSAY   I'm waiting Barrett, soon as me old yankee aunt dead,
some money going to fall to me.

BARRETT   Seem that all I catch in me hand is cow shit. I wish you
luck Lindsay. You deserve it. *(Pause)* Almost as much as
me. If you get to go to England Lindsay, before me, would
you send for me?

LINDSAY   Sure I send for you. You me countryman ain't you?

BARRETT   You a good man. If I get there first I would leave your
ass right here. *(Says this very offhand).*

LINDSAY   Me aunt can't live too much longer. I tell her I want to
go to England to study law or medicine or some bullshit.

BARRETT   You always have to tell a Jamaican you want to be a
Doctor or Lawyer or they leave you ass in hell. But

someday me going leave this place. This poor ass country where donkey hungry, where cow hungry, where man hungry. And I hungry – to rass.

Instant Darkness.

SCENE XI
ASPECTS OF TOWN

Study for Brothel . . . Nightworld

It is darkness. Knocking upon a door is heard; a metallic knock.

VOICE (WOMAN)   Who you want?

VOICE (MAN)   Miss Celestina, please.

VOICE (WOMAN)   Wait. *(Few seconds pass – another woman comes)*

CELESTINA   Who you is?

VOICE (MAN)   Rude Boy here, man.

CELESTINA   Take off them dark glass off you face so me can look you good. *(Pause)* All right, enter.

Lights come up

We find ourselves in a small bar with juke box, a stand for drinks behind which sits Miss Celestina, the mother superior of the whore house.

CELESTINA   Can't nobody know you in them dark shades boy. Keep them damn things off you eyes, you look like Mafia.

RUDE BOY   How you Miss Celestina?

CELESTINA   Suffering. Time hard man. The constables on me like peas on rice. *(She plays with the glasses she wears).* Well what you pleasure tonight? I have a white girl here from Holland.

RUDE BOY   No thanks, I don't favour them white girls.

CELESTINA   *(Looking at him in surprise)* You must be strange.

RUDE BOY   Yes, I strange, yes.

CELESTINA   Well, what you want drink?

RUDE BOY   I must drink something, right?

CELESTINA   This no yard, you know. You come here, you must spend money.

RUDE BOY   Give me some of that white rum there. *(She pours him drink)* Hold you water and lock up you daughter because Rude Boy here now.

He begins a systematic inspection of the different whores sitting around in their booths like girls in a charm school. Just then a light-skinned well-dressed glad boy type comes out of a room with an indian looking prostitute.

STANFORD   Come on baby *(Sings)* 'Gee but you're lovely' *(Turns to Celestina)* Give me two Appleton dark, Celestina.

CELESTINA   *(Smiling)* She sweet you, eh?

STANFORD   Yeah, very nice. No complaints. *(Laughing)* *(He notices Rude Boy who has already seen him and turned away)* Hey, Rude Boy!

RUDE BOY   Yeah, Man.

STANFORD   I was wondering where you was, haven't seen you for about a month man. What's happening?

RUDE BOY   Not too bad, you know.

STANFORD   Hey man, look here I'm going give you a jewel. *(Showing the girl off).* You want it.

RUDE BOY   *(Unimpressed)* No man, I don't want no coolie girl tonight. Want a woman black like me.

GIRL   *(Insulted)* You does favour lost dog. *(Walking away)*

STANFORD   Hold on baby, don't mind him, here buy some cigarettes. *(Gives her ten dollars)*

GIRL   Him too feisty. *(She leaves looking back at him over her shoulder)*

STANFORD   So what happens, why you have to do the girl like that?

RUDE BOY   Cool man, I just don't favour she.

STANFORD   Come on let me buy something. *(Turning to Celestina)* A cube of whites, Celestina.

RUDE BOY   I cool man, I drinking. *(Pause)* Hey man, remember that last time over your house.

STANFORD   Yeah man.

RUDE BOY   *(Very slowly)* Yeah man, you kind of hurt me you know.

STANFORD   How you mean?

RUDE BOY   Yeah man, we suppose to be big time friends and so. But you know when I was over your house the last time, and I was kind of talking to your sister Cathy . . .

STANFORD   Yeah.

RUDE BOY   Yeah man, well when your mother come in she kind of look at me as if I was a black dog you know. Cause she didn't like me talking to she daughter, 'cause she kind of red skin.

STANFORD   Hey man, listen . . .

RUDE BOY   Wait man, I talking. Then when you come in the room you kind of look strange upon me too. You know, as long as running whore house together and drawing ganja and so, everything cool. You like Rude Boy you know. Is me you send to buy you ganja. It's me yard you does come for smoke. But when I talk to you sister, then you come strange on me, 'cause you all is respectable people, right?

STANFORD   Wait man, wait. I was drunk that night that I don't even know self how I reach home.

RUDE BOY   Yeah that cool man. I know that you family them is big people, uncle in the Ministry, uncle in the army and all that shit. You can go all over the world. You got money in your pocket you never work hard a day in your life. Yet I know there is something you need from this Rude Boy here. You want soul and is me must give you. *(Stanford laughs.)* Yeah, you laugh, is cool man, is love.

STANFORD   Must be love, can't be but love.

RUDE BOY   Yes man, but I telling you here, don't come me yard no more, never.

STANFORD   Why, man?

RUDE BOY   Because I don't trust you man. You become Prime Minister if you want to. If tomorrow you want to be a police man you could but I, I just a rude boy and when them lash me just me blood would run.

STANFORD   What you mean, I don't want to be no police?

RUDE BOY   Hey man I can't trust you. I feel you could betray me. You is just one shade away from backra people. I a nigger man, I black, I dread.

STANFORD   Hey man, we used to be friends.

RUDE BOY   Man, what used to was, can't are.

STANFORD   All right man if that's how you feel.

RUDE BOY   That's the way of it man.

STANFORD   *(Turning to go then turns back)* Here man, I think I owe you this twenty.

RUDE BOY   No, cool man, hold you money.

   (Stanford walks off)

CELESTINA   Me don't care who is in power, PPP, P4P, PQP, if they don't give we food all the girls going end up working here for me, you watch.

RUDE BOY *(Turns to dark-skinned girl)* I think I favour you.

GIRL   You buying?

RUDE BOY   Most naturally.

GIRL   You must give she ten dollar for the room. *(Pointing to Celestina)*

RUDE BOY   Listen girl, I don't want none of that rubber jacket jive, I want ride you bareback.

GIRL   You forward you know. Feisty.

RUDE BOY   I want puss puss hard and straight, no chaser. *(The other whores laugh when they hear him say that)* Hold you water and lock up your daughter, because Rude Boy here now.

Darkness

SCENE XII
STUDY FOR ORGASM

Woman and her man in darkness

WOMAN   O Lord, Oh Lord, Oh Lord
Oy, Oy! Oy!
Oh Jesus, you must want kill me this night. Oh God it feel so good you must be drink strongback tea and turtle egg. You ram goat. Lord me back weak.

MAN   Airey. *(Stopping)*

WOMAN   Why you stop?

MAN   Thought you say me was hurting you.

WOMAN   Me tell you when to stop. Go on man. Forward man.

Oh Lord. Oh Lord!

Darkness

SCENE XIII
LA PUTA AND HER SISTER

She has skin like a dark East Indian, such as you might find in Trinidad, Aruba or Jamaica. She is too dark to be mulatto. Her mind is tired from a million encounters, all the same. Yet her body is too graceful to be common. Her eyes too full of information. Her sister Gogita is much lighter. They have the same father but different mothers. Her pain is the enclosed self-hate pain that light-skinned women have somewhere behind their eyes.

Afternoon. As scene opens La Puta is standing in the street laughing with a man. Gogita passes.

LA PUTA   You going bald Pepe, that wife of yours working you hard eh? *(She laughs)*

MAN   I must go home now. You going to be here for John Canoo?

LA PUTA   I'm going to be here yes, where I going?

MAN   More time yes!

LA PUTA   *(Looking at Gogita, runs after her)* You not going to speak to your sister kiddo?

GOGITA   *(Nervous)* Oh Lord, I didn't see you, how are you La Puta?

LA PUTA   You seen me. But it's all right. What you doing with yourself? You finish school?

GOGITA   Yes, I finished school, I'm teaching now.

LA PUTA   I did hear so yes, so you is a school teacher, you teach them how to read and write and salute the Queen and so.

GOGITA   What have you been doing?

LA PUTA   Surviving, I'm going survive.

GOGITA   You working?

LA PUTA   In a manner, yes. *(She laughs)* We does all work.

GOGITA   You look well.

LA PUTA   *(Looking her up and down)* You is a school teacher, yes you always was.

GOGITA   *(Taking her by the arm)* Look girl, why don't you do something with your life before you find yourself old?

LA PUTA   Do something like what, get married?

GOGITA   Do something besides . . .

LA PUTA   Besides what, pick up men? Say fuck, come say the word. You know the word? I just tease you. You know I like to tease you. You all right kiddo. How is you father?

GOGITA   You mean our father.

LA PUTA   He never did nothing for me but bring me into this world.

GOGITA   You should be grateful.

LA PUTA   For that?

GOGITA   That he brought you into his house.

LA PUTA   So what if he brought me into his house. The one with the good hair and the fair skin was you. The education, and all the love was always Gogita. You know I saw him last year in Barbados.

GOGITA   Who?

LA PUTA   You father. He didn't recognise me. He tried to pick me up.

GOGITA   You're lying.

LA PUTA   Of course you not going to believe me. I must be lying, yes. But I know he tried to put his hand up me dress. You can believe or not believe as you want to. And when I call his name, he turn frighten, and he see it was me and tears run from his eyes.

GOGITA   Sometimes I think the devil has you girl.

LA PUTA   The devil has me, and what about him. All men is the same. How long you think it takes to make a baby. I can make any man come in five minutes.

GOGITA   Girl have more respect for yourself than that.

LA PUTA   It takes five minutes to make a baby. That's all it takes to make a man a father. He drop he seed in a woman, like water in a well. And then he goes. And if he should meet his own child walking a night street he wouldn't know. They is all the same and you know is so. When a nigger man not hungry he wants a woman. When he have a woman then he want money.

GOGITA   Well if that's how you choose to believe then I can't stop you.

LA PUTA   How I choose to believe, and what about you, you sweet Harold who was going to marry you. Didn't he run off with a yankee woman just so he could go to America?

GOGITA   (Furious) You dirty bitch

LA PUTA   Lord, I didn't know you know such words. What would you school children say?

Gogita runs away. La Puta giggles like a little girl.

Darkness.

SCENE XIV
THE FATHER

The background of a dying evening. An evening of thin dark men and the bent women.

FATHER   Lindsay! Lindsay, you lazy-ass rebel! The boy so harden he wouldn't lift he hand not if donkey drop down in he lap. The boy a rebel yes. Me thought me bring a son into this world to be a comfort to me when I get old and can't find me way no more. But Lord know if I wait on that one to lead me I find me ass in a ditch. All he good for is to run with that other rasta Barrett and he sister who sell she ass to any man with a dollar in he hand. He think he aunt going to help him to go to England, boy got to be crazy. I remember when he was born, his mother say, 'Peter, me water bust'. He come up and he head big like a ripe coconut. Me did think something good was going to come from him – a baby with a head big so. I never meet a boy more chupid, he must be favour he mother. He don't come from me. All he good for is to give you loud talk about poems and what not else. Babylon go burn. Cho, he a rasta yes . . . and he does tief too. Next time he go gaol then naa let him go.

Darkness.

SCENE XV
STUDY FOR THE DAUGHTER

Saturday above Kingston

It is night. We are so high above Kingston that we can't even hear the barking dogs or see the flickering lights of the city. We are above on the road leading to Constance Gap, at the peak of a monstrous hill. It is Saturday night 12 o'clock. Those who live in the hills have worked like beast all week. They are the life blood of the city. They bring in the sugar cane, mangoes, bananas, coconuts. Their women

*bring in the labour force which keeps Kingston alive. Now it's night
and they party. The daughters dress in their bright colours. They
crowd into small bars on the side of the roads. They smell of deep
funk beneath their arms. Their bodies are strong and black. The
breast stand upward. The round nipples moving to God. Even the
twelve-year-old girls already have womanness on them. It's the time
of the moon, Virgo. And the bodies press hard to the rhythms of
Jonny Ace (Forever my Darling), Otis Redding (Your Precious
Love). Don Drummond (Heavenless). This is the day and the hour
of freedom. They have given all of the life force they could to the
city, now this time is for them.*

SCENE XVI
THE LEAVING OF JAMAICA

*Lindsay takes Barret to one side and whispers to him. On stage a
rasta band is playing* Rasta Man Come From Zion.

BARRETT   So what happen man? Why you pull me away when I
was just about to chat up that young daughter? Me feel say
she ready, you know. The younger the cherry the tighter the
squeeze.

LINDSAY   Listen man, me money reach. Me aunt send for me.

BARRETT   You too lie. For True?

LINDSAY   She send it, I tell you.

BARRETT   So you a reach a England before me eh? Well I glad
for you anyhow. Come, we must get black-up for the last.

LINDSAY   No man, I just want move quiet like a thief. You know
how these people be. Just like crabs in a barrel, them not
happy for you when them see you do too well. Them just
want for pull you back down again. I go just left quiet, you
no see it?

BARRETT   Sight brother. But look, you better let me hold a ten for you here just so that if you money run out in a England you could check me for help *(Lindsay gives him some money to hold for him)*. Cool.

LINDSAY   I want you write me and tell me how me people going.

BARRETT   Don't worry, I man can't write like you but I keep in touch. You just watch that you don't come like Elijah. He left for England and when he come back home he was mad as ass. Mind!

LINDSAY   Don't worry. *(Hugging him)* I going right.

BARRETT   *(Looking deep inside Lindsay and holding back everything he wants to say to him)* Send for me Lindsay. Send for me.

Barrett returns to the group and watches and Lindsay vanishes.

Darkness.

ACT II
ENGLAND

SCENE I

England

Lindsay visits family at Notting Hill Gate

LINDSAY   *(Walks about stage, addresses audience).* Notting Hill
Gate . . . used to be called Rotting Hill, a coal dump.
Inhabited now by West Indians and the poor whites.
(Knocks on door) Hello in there.

VOICE INSIDE   What do you want? Who do you want to see?

LINDSAY   Is a Mrs. Ethel Barzy within?

VOICE INSIDE   Ethel . . . it's for you *(Door opens)*

LINDSAY   Hello. I'm Lindsay Thomas's son.

AUNT ETHEL   *(An immense West Indian woman with a free
laugh, massive arms upon which dangle several bracelets).*
Oh, me Lord, it's Lindsay. Come in, come in son. Let me
see you. Walter, Joyce . . . come it's Thomas's boy, Lindsay.
When you arrive in London?

LINDSAY   Er . . . a few days ago.

AUNT ETHEL   And you didn't come see us until now?

LINDSAY   Well, I was, um . . . trying to get myself situated.

> *Enter Walter and Joyce. Walter is a well-built West Indian in
> his twenties and he looks like a labourer. Joyce is an attrac-
> tive brown-skinned, straight-haired West Indian girl who
> looks about nineteen. The third person to emerge
> eventually is Peter Barzy, the husband of Ethel. He is about
> forty-seven, well-built and in manner, like a skilled carpenter,
> sure and steady.*

AUNT ETHEL   Walter, do you remember Lindsay? You were just boys when we left for England.

WALTER   Yes, I remember, I used to lick him up all the time *(Laughs)*. How are you man?

LINDSAY   I'm still alive, I guess. *(Looks very intently at Joyce)*.

AUNT ETHEL   This is Joyce Donoway, my niece. She just arrived from Barbados last November.

JOYCE   My pleasure.

LINDSAY   You have extraordinary eyes, Joyce.

JOYCE   They're just eyes. I use them to see through.

LINDSAY   Oh, how interesting.

AUNT ETHEL   Peter, come and see little Lindsay.

PETER   Well, he not little no more. He's a full grown man. How are you doing boy? Pull down you pants, let me see how old you is.

AUNT ETHEL   Well, you must come eat with us Walter, get another chair from the bedroom there *(She always indicates)*.

WALTER   Yes, of course.

AUNT ETHEL   Let me take your coat.

LINDSAY   Thank you.

Joyce walks on and off stage as she sets table.

AUNT ETHEL   Where are you staying?

LINDSAY   Near Holland Park.

AUNT ETHEL   Oh, not far. It's just there so.

PETER   You plan on staying on in London?

LINDSAY   I don't know. I haven't been able to come to sense about this place yet. I think I like Scotland.

WALTER   I've been to Scotland, it's too cold there, man. It's always raining.

LINDSAY   Yes, but I think they have better places of learning.

WALTER   Oh, you're studying something?

PETER   Yes, his father always say, he the one with the books.

LINDSAY   Yes, well . . . I'm not studying as such. I mean, I write, poetry in fact, I've been doing that for several years now.

PETER   And what you do for a living?

LINDSAY   I write poetry.

PETER   What? *(Incredously)* You mean all you does do is write. That's a good life there boy. A poet.

LINDSAY   Yes.

JOYCE   *(Entering)* What's strange about being a poet? *(Puts down plate)*

LINDSAY   Thank you.

PETER   Yes, you right, it's not that I believe there is anything wrong with this writer thing, but . . . um it seems to me that a black man would have a great deal of trouble. Do you know what I mean?

LINDSAY   Yes, you're right.

PETER   I know.

WALTER   I don't believe in all of that. I mean books is good but in England what you need is a trade, understand me. If you can do things with your hands . . .

PETER   And if you know the right people.

WALTER   Yes . . . well . . . most naturally the right people too. That's always necessary if you have these things in England, you can survive, understand me.

LINDSAY   And, of course, it helps considerably to not be West Indian.

WALTER   *(Laughs)* Yes, true. Don't be West Indian if you can help it.

PETER   *(Seating himself before long table)* Ten years ago it wasn't so bad.

AUNT ETHEL   Joyce, bring in the yams and the peas when you come in girl. *(Exit Joyce)* Lord, I'm so tired these days that I forget everything. Close the curtains there for me, Walter. *Walter rises and goes to close curtains, Joyce enters with two filled bowls.*

JOYCE   Here you are then, Aunt Ethel.

AUNT ETHEL   You shut off the stove?

JOYCE   Yes.

AUNT ETHEL   Hand me me sweater there. I'm still cold, can't get use to this country, buddy.

LINDSAY   Yes, it's cold.

PETER   When I first come here, my first winter, you know. Lord . . . I wear me puddin-drawers and three sweaters, with a . . . what you call them shirts?

WALTER   Flannel shirts.

PETER   Yes, flannel shirts, a scarf and a heavy coat and cap, and me still was cold. Me ears burn me man. I say, but Jesus why you sent me here?

WALTER   Yes, your ears burn you, yes. *(They all laugh)*

LINDSAY   *(Turning to Joyce who is seated beside him)* You have beautiful legs, Joyce.

JOYCE   Thank you. *(Trying to seem unmoved)* I dance.

LINDSAY   Oh yes.

JOYCE   Classical, mainly.

AUNT ETHEL   Yes, she's a very fine dancer. She wants to dance
with the Royal Ballet some day.

LINDSAY   The Royal Ballet, *(almost childishly)* yeah?

JOYCE   You don't have to tell everyone, auntie. Yes, I want to
dance with them. I will some day.

WALTER   You going to be the first black face in there, eh, Joyce
Ann? *(Laughs like a hyena)*

JOYCE   It has to happen, and when it does, I'll be ready. *(Jumps
up from the table and goes off stage to kitchen)*

AUNT ETHEL   *(To Lindsay)* Walter, don't you make sport of her
dancing any more. She works so hard. She comes from her
job, she works at the tubes at Oxford Circus. And she
comes home, eats and goes right out again to class. Four
times a week.

PETER   She'll make it if she keep it up.

WALTER   I only joking, I know she's a good dancer.

PETER   That's a real West Indian woman there, she sure has a
strong will.

Joyce re-enters with salt shaker in hand.

AUNT ETHEL   Well. let's say grace.

LINDSAY   .*(Leaning toward Joyce)* Do you ever go out on dates,
love?

JOYCE   No.

LINDSAY   Would you like to?

JOYCE   No.

LINDSAY   Oh!

PETER   Lindsay, why don't you lead us in prayer, you're the one that knows so many words.

LINDSAY   *(Startled at first, then relaxes)* All right. *(Rises)* God
bless this house and all that's within
And God keep us all away from sin
Keep out the night the streets and the damp
The black poet who lives by grace and by thanks
The rastaman, the scribe and the priest
And may all at this table love increase. Amen.

AUNT ETHEL   Why thank you Lindsay.

PETER   Yes, he good. He did always love words anyhow. He does favour Vinrick.

WALTER   Didn't they say Vinrick is in a mad house in Tooting Bec?

Aunt Ethel looks at Walter disapprovingly, he catches himself.

AUNT ETHEL   Well, let's eat.

They finish eating.

JOYCE   *(To Lindsay)* That was very good.

LINDSAY   I like you, you know?

JOYCE   I'm glad . . . I think.

Dissolves to Joyce's monologue.

Monologue

JOYCE   *(Dresses a small brown skin doll while she is speaking)* So
they sent me to boarding school in Antigua, to study
French and Latin and piano. And they had to pay two
pounds ten extra a term for piano. And when I was sixteen,
Lloyd led me to a grove. And when I asked him if it was
right he said that it was all right and that only the stars
would know. And other girls had gone there. When I found

I was pregnant, Lloyd went away to Dominica and my belly swelled like the mouths of the old gossiping women.
So my people took the baby from me and sent me away to England. Now I'm here in another city and men do not take their women into groves but into apartments instead, with doors that shut tight after them. And now no mouths whisper.

Dissolves back to

LINDSAY   I'll come see you when you dance with the Royal Ballet.

JOYCE   All right.

LINDSAY   I would like very much, I think . . .

JOYCE   What?

LINDSAY   To stick my tongue in your ear.

JOYCE   *(Quietly)* Don't say that.

LINDSAY   Why?

JOYCE   Because that's not nice.

LINDSAY   Oh, sorry.

Turns and sees Peter

Darkness

SCENE II
LA PUTA AND BARRETT IN ENGLAND

BARRETT   *(Carrying two bags)* You see how he was looking at you?

LA PUTA   Who was looking?

BARRETT   The Australian cross the hall.

LA PUTA   I didn't even notice him.

BARRETT   England's going be good for us, you watch.

LA PUTA   I don't like this place.

BARRETT   That 'cause you just come. Let me hold some money, I'm going see some of my contacts.

LA PUTA   Don't chat you shit now, I know you, remember.

BARRETT   What you mean you know me? This serious business I talking here now.

LA PUTA   All the time you asking me for money, where I going get it from?

BARRETT   What about you Doctor?

LA PUTA   You must be drunk, I can't keep going to him so, he get tired.

BARRETT   Never mind, I going take care of it. I going sell some of this herb.

LA PUTA   You know the people here?

BARRETT   I got contacts.

LA PUTA   Oh ho. They lock you rass up here, you know.

BARRETT   Serious, I just need something to start. Cast your bread upon the waters and at the end of many days it shall return to you.

LA PUTA   So them say.

BARRETT   You going to have to have faith in you brother. You never think we reach this England, but I fix you up didn't I?

LA PUTA   You me brother, yes, but you a man and a man does tief. *(Pause)* You tief me yes. *(She reaches in purse and gives him five pounds)*

BARRETT   *(Reaching for money)* Don't worry, we going do good here.

The action of taking money is frozen . . . Darkness

SCENE III
LINDSAY AND THE AFRICAN

*Lindsay is looking in the gutters for money. He stumbles in the
streets, he is in a kind of drug stupour. A South African helps him to
his feet.*

AFRICAN   Are you all right?

LINDSAY   Yes, I'm okay.

AFRICAN   You're from South Africa?

LINDSAY   No.

AFRICAN   Ethiopia . . . Nigeria?

LINDSAY   The West Indies but . . . *(the African lets go of his arm
and lets him fall)*

AFRICAN   I thought you were a South African. *(exits)*

LINDSAY   Lord, if you should turn your face against me
Wouldn't I be like these the others
Shango boys among broken dice?
Lord, if you should turn your face against me
Wouldn't I just fall in this street and dead
If you should turn
Your face
Against
Me.

Darkness

LICK AND LOVE
To Drumming
More times I feel sorry
More time I feel sad
But yet I try to keep my sorrow
Inside my own private world.

Is mostly when we lick and love girl

Rub-up all night
Is mostly when we lick and love
That I feel all right.

We are children of sugar
We are children of Cain
We are children of Judah
We are children of pain.

I glad you come a England girl
I'm well glad you reach
I just hope you can hold
All that this place has to teach.

Long as money last girl
Things not so bad
It's when the money done girl
Is then they want drive you mad.

Is like you waiting for summer
And no summer come
Is like you searching summer
But no summer a come.

SCENE IV
AUNT ETHEL AND LONDON TRANSPORT

Aunt Ethel who is working as a ticket collector for London Transport. The day is Sunday.

(Singing)

AUNT ETHEL   This is my story, this is my song
          Praising my saviour all the day long
          God forgive me and pardon me for working on your day.
          The spirit is willing to sacrifice but the flesh is weak.
          Tickets please. *(Sees Barrett who is trying to slip past)*
          Excuse me, ticket please!

BARRETT   Oh listen, I not going to ride. I just go look see if there's any loose change on the platform. *(Runs on)*

AUNT ETHEL   But look the cheek no, he just want see if there's any loose change. I bet you me call the police after you.

Darkness

Enter Barrett who finds Lindsay nodding in a stupour. The location is Soho in London

BARRETT   Lindsay! Come on, man, you no change so. Help yourself up.

LINDSAY   Barrett, you not Barrett?

BARRETT   I'm Barrett, yes, if you is Lindsay, I'm Barrett. You lucky I recognize you by that big coconut head of yours.

LINDSAY   It's been so long man . . . I'm not Lindsay no more.

BARRETT   You Lindsay, yes. I thought you was going to send for me.

LINDSAY   I wanted to but . . .

BARRETT   You come all the way to white man's England to become a dopey.

LINDSAY   I'm not . . .

BARRETT   You is a dopey yes. We hear back home what you been doing.

LINDSAY   Barrett I take dope so I don't kill somebody.

BARRETT   You killing yourself man. But I'm not here to judge you.

LINDSAY   How did you get over?

BARRETT   Me sister.

LINDSAY   La Puta?

BARRETT   La Puta yes, she got an Englishman by the nose. He give her a thousand pounds.

LINDSAY   A thousand pounds?

BARRETT   See man, the scene is different than back home.

LINDSAY   I see so.

BARRETT   See, but you going to have to understand these British girls is funny. They want you mash them up sometimes so that they 'fraid you. Bite them hard on they tittie and so.

LINDSAY   They like Babylon.

BARRETT   All that kind of jive, what you do is give them what they want. Who they want you be, you be so.

LINDSAY   How these people so?

BARRETT   I don't know, I ain't no doctor. Must be the weather here. The women like devils. That's why I know sis could do good business here man. Englishman 'fraid him woman. We could make big money.

LINDSAY   These people here is the Corinthians man. *(They laugh)*

BARRETT   So tell me here how you fall to this dope thing.

LINDSAY   I don't want talk 'bout that . . .

BARRETT   It's nothing to me man, I just want know how this thing come on you.

LINDSAY   Was a night like so. Streets were darkness. You hearing me good?

BARRETT   I hearing you.

LINDSAY   And I hungry bad man. I walking down into the tubes at Knightsbridge. Me legs come weak on me and the stairs come up to me like I dreaming I thought I dead. *(Barrett laughs)* You think I joke? When I wake up I find I in a hospital. I meet up with some fellows there who start me into this thing. They tell me it easy here because the

Government give it to you.

BARRETT   Sure they give it to you, they want you stay on that shit.

LINDSAY   I can't walk down there by the Thames. I see blood in
that water. Water full of blood. Sometimes I look so and I
see death, I look so and I see death, and I look back so
again. You understand what I saying?

BARRETT   I understand what you saying. Come on go home.

LINDSAY   I can't leave this England yet man, I must find something more than I come over with, if it's one thing, sight?

BARRETT   Seen Brother, seen.

Darkness

SCENE V
LA PUTA IN ISLINGTON PUB

*She has now been in London a year. The city has carved anonymity
on her once beautiful face. She is seated in a pub drinking
Babycham and Vodka.*

LA PUTA   Riddle me riddle, guess me this riddle and perhaps not.
What am I doing here anyway? Thought this England was
going to be different. Well it's different all right. *(Sucks her
teeth)* Me friends back home jealous after me because I get
to come here. *(She mimicks them)* 'La Puta reach up top.
She gone a high England'. They think this place paradise.
Mek they come here no, if they want see what paradise
give. This place no easy brother. I tell you. For eleven
months is pure winter I see. Can't find summer yet. This
place. People them cooking in they house and you can't
even smell not a thing. Them call this life. People sit in the
trains here just dead from the neck up. Heads just bury
inside a newspaper. And if you black, them don't even want
to sit by you.

Great Britain, you sure ain't great no more. Me could tell you that. Can't even take a chance at night. People here love for rape-up and chop-up on pickney, never mind woman.

And this man friend I got now. He a next one again. He just want see me on a Thursday. Fraid him woman catch him out in a lie. I should care, just make sure he gives me some money when we done. I don't care for no man really, even me brother Barrett spend all he time in the betting shop. Mecca, them call it. 'Sis I go make a pilgrimage to Mecca'. When he come home not a damn thing in he pocket but dust.

There was just one man I love back home. Solo. He use to ask me: 'Girl, why you look so sad with them wild doe eyes? Come mek we lively-up weself. What is it you dreaming after?'

I dreaming of a man who could do for me what I can't do for meself. A man who would say let go all your suffering and misery and see with me.

PUB OWNER   *(Ringing bell)* Last orders please.

LA PUTA   Solo, why you have to kill yourself in some car. You always love to drive wild and what it get you. You man so foolish I should just laugh after you. Nigger man always must prove something. Now you dead and what me for do?

PUB OWNER   Last orders please. Come on drink up.

LA PUTA   Shut you bati-hole no man. Shut you damn bati-hole. What do you?

People here love for rush you in this England. Can't see with this place no more. Must try send for me daughter. Take she from bush. Auntie love for give she too much licks. Try and reach The States. Mek a better chance there. Lord help me find a way.

Riddle me riddle, guess me this riddle and perhaps not.

Darkness

SCENE VI
STUDY FOR WATCHMAN IN YOUTH CENTRE

*He is over fifty and seated before a television set. He drinks his Mt.
Gay rum to punctuate his thoughts. In the background a group of
young West Indians are drinking and playing dominoes loudly. This
is Lindsay's Uncle Peter*

UNCLE PETER   I don't know why these youths keep so much
noise about the place. All they study is wickedness and
gangsterism. They say England hard for them now. They
should have come here twenty years ago then they would
know what hardness give. I come here with not a Jesus
thing except me two long arms them, you hear me? At that
time not a union, not a taxi-cab, not a man want to see you
if you black. It was hard then for true, but the family pull
weself together and we make it. We form a sou-sou. We
collect the money from all the different families from back
home. One week I get it, next week you get it. In that way
we could survive since Lloyd's Bank don't want see no
black face. But as for these nasty-ass young people them,
they should just line them up and shoot them one time.
They no damn good. They would thief you damn eye out
you head if you don't watch good. *(Takes drink)*
Now my son come tell me I should go join union. For
what? Let them who want traffic with politics go on. I all
right. I cool. I have a house, I mean it old but then I old. I
have a colour telly, what more could a man ask? People tell
me I should go back home. What I going home for? I don't
even have pot for self piss in, back home. People chuppid.
I'll tell anybody England make me what I am today. You
hear me? England make me what I am today.

*Slow darkness as the youth laugh at him, The Broken
Generation*

SCENE VII
THE GOSPEL OF RASTAFARI

Lindsay, the Leaving of London

LINDSAY   And so the prophecy was fulfilled. The old men dream
their dreams but only the young men shall dream visions.
And so, don't feel that you know me because you don't.
I move through this England like sunlight cutting through
darkness. This same land where Garvey died in his exile.
This same England where Nkrumah had to search dustbin
for food.
To fulfill a prophecy: 'One shall come to make the others
remember'.
And Edward the Prince, did go to Ethiopia, to bring back to
Selassie the Rod of Correction which the Ita-lia-ns had
stolen. And when he reached Ethiopia, Edward did wander
in the fields and did eat grass like Nebuchezar of Babylon,
because he was Babylon.
And Eli-abeth, who they call Queen, shall bear a son who
will be the last King of Babylon to sit upon the throne at its
end.
And these things will come to pass in *your* time. For a truth.
And so I pass through this place like sunlight cutting
through darkness. This England where black man walk with
heel mash down and soul mash down. This England where
Garvey died and Nkrumah had to search dustbin for food.
And who here knows I?

ACT III
AMERICA

SCENE I
THE ENTRANCE TO AMERICA

Kennedy Airport. Lindsay is greeted by his cousin Clayton whom he has not seen in over seven years.

CLAYTON   Hey Lindsay, over here.

LINDSAY   Cousin Clayton, how you going man?

CLAYTON   Not too bad. You still have the same baby face. What all that hair doing on you head. You trying to come Rasta now?

LINDSAY   You look good cousin Clayton. Put on weight, life must be sweet.

CLAYTON   Well, trying. How was your trip over? You like flying?

LINDSAY   Not bad. I fly before. *(Looks around)* Just a moment. Oh that's not her. I thought it was that airline stewardess. She have some fit legs 'pon she, boy.

CLAYTON   If you don't have no money you may as well forget her. This not back home now. Money talks and bullshit walks.

LINDSAY   So this is New York. This is where Rockerfeller and the rest of them big boys print up money on they machine when they ready. I don't 'fraid this place you know, not after London.

CLAYTON   Oh yeah. You have some place to stay?

LINDSAY   Well no, I thought you . . .

CLAYTON   Well my wife is away in Toronto for a few weeks. You can stay with me for a while until she comes back anyway.

LINDSAY   That will be cool. I'll soon force something together.
What kind of work West Indians do here?

CLAYTON   Drive a cab, or work as guards. Can you count well?

LINDSAY   Sure I can count. You joke.

CLAYTON   We'll see what we can find for you.

LINDSAY   What you do cousin Clayton?

CLAYTON   Me, I'm a Tax Consultant and a landlord . . . I haven't
any vacancies at the moment though.

LINDSAY   Oh.

CLAYTON   Well come on, my car is outside.

LINDSAY   New York New York. So nice they named it twice.

*Lindsay touches his fingers to his lips and then touches the
ground. Clayton looks at him and laughs.*

Darkness

SCENE II

A letter to Lindsay's father

LINDSAY   *(Addresses audience)* Father, as you know it's a long
time now since I break away. It seems a long time now since
I've gone. I've seen a lot of things. Sorrow, pain and suffera-
tion. Your son is not afraid just sometimes I feel so alone.
The Englishman smiles at you as he cuts your black throat.
The American won't even bother to smile as he does it.
They at least are more honest. You know how back home
the donkey and the goat labour with a rope around their
neck. They never question why, they only labour until they
drop. Well your son don't want for dead so. Too many
West Indians dead from labour, father. That is why I had to
break away.

I love you as I love my mother. I know both of you try to
make me see. There are things I never said because the
world got in the way. Forgive me my silence.

I'm going to try my best and send something for you by Jan
Canoo. Pray for me. Your one son, Lindsay.

Enter Cousin Clayton, irritated.

CLAYTON   Hey Lindsay, I want to talk to you for a minute.

LINDSAY   Sure man, I was just writing my father.

CLAYTON   Yeah, that's good. Nothing wrong with that. Look
man I just want to know what your intentions are?

LINDSAY   My intentions?

CLAYTON   Yeah, you agreed to pay twenty-five dollars a week for
the room. That's fair. Now every week it's a story and I just
want to know what the hell is going on.

LINDSAY   Look man, I've been trying to find work.

CLAYTON   Well that's not good enough. All I see you doing is
laying around the apartment, smoking that stuff and putting
up pictures of Selassie on the walls. This ain't no damn
club house, you know.

LINDSAY   I try that fellow Jacobs you send me to. And what come
of it? I think that he's a bati-man anyhow. I can't deal with
them people. This place just come like a nightmare to me, I
can't believe it real.

CLAYTON   Well you better wake from that dream, brother,
because at the end of the week your ass is going the hell
out of here. Look man, I'm sorry for you but I've got
problems of my own to deal with. This is America. Things
move fast here. You come here to work, not to live. After
you make some money then you can go home and live. So
you better get it together quick fast and in a hurry. You got
until the end of the week.

LINDSAY   Man, kiss out me bloodseed!

Darkness

SCENE III
STUDY FOR PIPER, THE GOOD SON

About thirty-five, short and stocky like a Badian, eyes which say no harm. Face which is clear because it keeps its earth close.

PIPER   Get your curry goat, roti here. Ginger beer and mauby. *(As if continuing conversation)* . . . But you see, when you come from hardness, you does expect the worse and you not surprised when it befall you. Now I had seven brothers and sisters and I was the darkest because I was a child of the first marriage. And I would have to wait on the other six to eat before I could eat. I would have to wait on the leavings of their plate because of that mulatto bastard who they call John Hunter, my stepfather. God forgive me for calling him so, but so he be, and wherever he is this night, may dog eat his supper. He treat me mother bad, because the devil come on him when he drunk. So, as soon as I meet up with a way to leave home, I gone. I live with my cousin Baily and I first come here and he get me a job where he work there on Fourteenth Street. And we working for a Jew man name of Goldstein, and he sell furniture and carpet and so. Now this cousin Baily thieving this Jew man for ten years. Every time the man gone, Baily selling this friend and that friend and not putting nothing down in no book.
There was a Haitian girl who answer phone there at this place. What's her name now? . . . Monique. Anyway, this girl never talk to me, for five months she look at me as if I stone or water. Until one day she see this Goldstein put his hand on me shoulder and telling me 'You a good worker, Piper, I could see that you like your cousin Baily. You going work long time for me'. Now she like that you know. All of

a sudden it's 'Hello Piper, how you this morning?' *(Nods head in understanding of what life is all about. The actor must give the audience time to follow him in this awareness)*

Bitch! But you know, a feeling come on me, I feel to meself that I don't want be like my cousin Baily, I don't want work for no man for no ten years. Even you tiefing him, he still making profit on you, and he always know what you trying to hide. I want be my own man. I never go back there. I guess I funny so.

. . . Curry goat . . . Roti, get your ginger beer . . .

Darkness

SCENE IV
MASTER AND SLAVE

MASTER   I don't understand you, nigger. I take your money away from you and you survive. I take away your language and you make another one. I stick you in concrete and you even make that a home. I kill you and I kill you and yet you always survive. *(Facing audience)* I don't understand you, nigger.

Darkness

THE WEST INDIAN JUST HIT NEW YORK

LINDSAY   *(Singing)*

Nobody going to run me from where me come from.
Rasclaat, this New York City. Can't tell the people from the garbage.
I going to get me a car. Watch me. Soon as I get me a job.
I going get cadillac car. I going make it here you know.
It hard for true, but I going make it. I don't give a damn.
They does have power but they only a man like me.
I going get me a job yes. I don't want do it but I can do if I have to.

(He sees girl passing)

Hello there, Miss White Pants!

GIRL   Hello, who are you?

LINDSAY   The 'Cisco Kid, and you are my sister and my queen.

GIRL   I can't be your sister, I'm Portuguese. You not my family.

LINDSAY   Well you is in New York now and you ain't Portuguese.
Stop your dreaming. You understand me, when things
come up hard for me is going go hard for you. So you best
let go of all that jive. I don't care if you is Portuguese or
Jamaican or Bajan or Haitian. You might just as cheap
hold that to yourself cause here they just have one name
for you: NIGGER! And you does walk graveyard like me.

She storms away angry.

Darkness

SCENE V
HILDA'S SOLILOQUY

HILDA   *(As though continuing conversation)* . . . And at that time I
was very young and what I thought I knew I did not know.
But I was young and in my father's house and when he
called me by name, I would come.
. . . When I was sixteen I work in the market with me mother
when I could. We have our little stand there by the edge of
the road and we sell cookies and tarts and sugar cane.
Sometimes we sell wildroot and arrowroot and other herbs
that you does get to sweat you when you sick.
And at the time I was in love with this boy name Edmund,
and I love him bad, bad, you know, but my mother had turn
her face against him because she say he lazy and he had
make a baby with this girl Fufu who live by Donkey Walk.
When was it now? *(Thinks for a moment)* It must have

been during Lent, I met this Englishman name of Derek
and he was a soldier I would go for walks with him, you
know, and he give me little presents and so. Well, Edmund
come to me house one night and he so calm, calm, you
never know what in his mind.

'I hear you seeing some Englishman, a white soldier?' Yes, I
say, I know a soldier, Uhmmmm and he does buy you
things no?' Yes, he buy me little things, he bring me a
mirror so I could see meself in the morning.

Then with no warning, he bust me such a slap across me
face that me ears start ring. I never see more stars.

'You not going to be no white man's woman, before I see
you so I break you damn back. And you tell you
Englishman that if I catch him trouble you again, I cut him
rass.'

I just sit and cry, I don't say nothing to him because he
might mash up me mouth. Lord that man had a temper,
(laughs) but I never see that Englishman again. (Pause)
Now I have this cousin name of Kafa, we call him cousin,
so much family I does hardly know who is cousin from who
isn't. Anyway this cousin Kafa did have a twist foot. You
know his foot turn so. (She demonstrates) His have vision
and so, he say that spirit talk to him.

He tell me Hilda, you going to go on a long journey and
death will be all around you but won't touch you. And he
make me frighten you know. Me don't like to hear people
talk like that.

And then me mother was very sick, and I used to cook for
her. But she told me that I would have to leave and go
away to live with her sister in America. And I didn't want to
leave, and she send me away on the sea and I never felt
more sick. And beneath me is all black water and when I
come to New York I so cold. And when I meet me aunt, I
sit down with her and I take her hand and I say, Nana, what
should I do to go well In America? and she say 'White
people here is as white people all over the world. And if
you cook for them and see after they children, you'll do

good.' And the very first job I get I held for twenty years. I come when they children was small and I stay until their children grow and have child of they own. I watch they children, I scrub they floors, I cook . . . and when the old woman dies *(pause)* they leave me fifty dollars.

(She laughs)

Fifty dollars. Then I understand. If you work until you drop you will never do enough for white people. And if you waiting on their kindness then, buddy, dog eat you supper. All those years and they never raise my wage. But me no trouble meself no more because it don't make sense. They think God bring you into the world to be servant for them. But it can't remain so forever. Nothing stay so forever.

(She starts to walk off)

Because I remember when I was young and in my father's house.

Darkness

SCENE VI
STUDY FOR OLD GARVEYITE

HAROLD   I have this pain bad in me chest, I don't think I open the store today. Let me sit down here . . . tired.

WIFE   The Doctor tell you not to trouble up you self you know. I can take care of the store.

HAROLD   O Anne, please. *(disgusted)* You can't even take care of yourself how you going to take care of store. I don't know what you going do when I die.

WIFE   Don't talk so.

HAROLD   When I come here in '41, the only fear I have is that I might die poor and they have to bury me in Potter's Field.

WIFE   You don't have to bury in Potter's Field now.

HAROLD   I know that's why I'm not frighten. *(Knock at door)*

WIFE   Is you nephew. *(She lets him in)*

HAROLD   Oh Lord.

LINDSAY   How you doing, Uncle Harold? *(Kisses aunt)*

WIFE   But you don't know what a comb for, right? Why you hair so tall?

LINDSAY   *(To uncle)* You look good.

HAROLD   He must be want something. This boy here a cross to me.

LINDSAY   I don't want nothing. I just come see you.

WIFE   You hungry?

LINDSAY   A little peckish yes.

HAROLD   Uhmmmm

WIFE   *(Laughing)* You not really hungry but you could eat right? I fix you something. *(exits)*

HAROLD   But what's the matter with you boy, you don't make up you mind to do nothing at all at all. But how you could be so? You young. If I had you strength I work three jobs. Why you don't make you some money?

LINDSAY   I think this money thing is bad for you. It does get people very vex, and there should be enough for everybody.

HAROLD   You talk like Garvey. When I did first come here I did think so too. But he did trust people too much and they betray him.

LINDSAY   Because of that same money.

HAROLD   Don't chat shit, what can you do without money 'cept make baby, that's all you good for anyway. When I was you age I had two jobs, I hold on to both of them for fifteen years. That's right. You make you bed hard you lay in it hard. You must put something away, you can't stay so forever you know.

LINDSAY   But what I work so for?

HAROLD   What you mean what you going to work so for, so that you don't end up in Potter's Field. I work fifteen years for Horn and Hardart, and I keep my own restaurant at night. For fifteen years.

LINDSAY   You a good man, uncle.

HAROLD   Buck up yourself boy if you got a good job where they need you, when you can do something no one else can do. Like take me now, I cook all them years for them at Hardart's and I never tell them the secret to me gravy recipes. And they try and thief it you know, but I never tell them a damn thing. You see they did need me. You laugh! You take it for a damn joke. They'll bury you in Potter's Field.

LINDSAY   Then my spirit will walk the earth.

WIFE   *(Returning)* What you doing argue with the boy, Harold? The Doctor tell you don't trouble yourself you know.

HAROLD   *(Sitting down)* Spirit walk the earth! Somebody should cuff him in he damn head. The boy ignorant.

WIFE   You know he don't have good sense.

HAROLD   I does forget sometimes. *(Has a heart attack.)* Oh, God! Me chest.

WIFE   Harold!

Darkness

SCENE VII
LINDSAY MEETS BARRETT IN NEW YORK

The place is a record shop on Nostrand Avenue in Brooklyn

LINDSAY   Barrett, Barrett, come here man, is Lindsay. Come.

BARRETT   Raated, Lindsay, if you know how I search for you.
              What happening? You working here?

LINDSAY   Yeah, still struggling but everything is just for a while,
              until I can do better.

BARRETT   I ask you Cousin Clayton for you. He say he don't
              know if you alive or dead.

LINDSAY   How you sister, La Puta?

BARRETT   La Puta turn Christian now, she say she find God.

LINDSAY   What, La Puta turn Christian?

BARRETT   So it be. She say you mustn't call she La Puta no
              more. She's Lilly, now.

LINDSAY   Bumboclaat!

BARRETT   She studying for come a nurse. She sending for she
              daughter and thing. So how the man keeping?

LINDSAY   Same way, but I learn a lot of things here in this
              America. It's hard for true and drier than dry, but still I
              learn.

BARRETT   You feel it easy to thief money here. There's more
              than London that's for true.

LINDSAY   I feel I want to write a book with me name on it. You
              understand? I want to write about how everybody own us
              but ourselves.

BARRETT   You still with that book business. People don't want
              know about nothing too serious, they still want to deal with
              Anansi stories.

LINDSAY   I always feel like white people using us but I didn't know how. Now I know how and why.

BARRETT   Is a dangerous knowledge that. When you come too wise you can't go back home again because they lick you down.

LINDSAY   I can't waste time with fear anymore.

BARRETT   Them say Jerusalem does slay its prophets. Mind.

LINDSAY   You see the way we does always come together, you and I. No matter how hard they try to separate we. That's why I'm not afraid.

BARRETT   I'm going get La Puta. She's just up the road. I soon come.

Darkness

SCENE VIII
LINDSAY AND LA PUTA

LA PUTA   *(Singing)*
Reel and turn me
Me say, me say reel and turn me
You want me go fall down
Break me belly upon tambourine

LINDSAY   So you come Christian, Lilly?

LA PUTA   You want laugh after me, right?

LINDSAY   I not laughing. I just wonder that's all.

LA PUTA   And what is it you does believe in?

LINDSAY   Me, I believe in Rastafari.

LA PUTA   They say Selassie wouldn't deal with us. We were too black for him. He only want the Ethiopians.

LINDSAY   Is not the man I believe in. Is the presence of the man.

He can trace his ancestry to black Solomon. We need a
past so we can know our future. And what do you believe
in?

LA PUTA   I believe in Jesus.

LINDSAY   Well I man believe in the same thing. Jesus was a black
man who looked upon the might of Rome and became
excited. Not afraid, just excited. He build the strongest faith
the world had ever known. So you see we believe the same.
So come love me no.

LA PUTA   You just want trouble me. Rub-me-up and left me.

LINDSAY   No, I want to love you. Maybe love my way out of
bondage.

LA PUTA   *(Smiling)* You always have the words Lindsay.
Reel and turn me
Me say, me say reel and turn me
You want me go fall down
Break me belly upon tambourine.

Slow darkness

SCENE IX
UNCLE HAROLD AND THE HISTORY OF RASTAFARI

UNCLE HAROLD   *(Reading from Bible)* I had fainted if I had not
believed. *(Pauses to think about this)* Lord knows that's
true enough. They drove us from the desert to the sea. We
who follow Garvey. Because he say that the Black man
should stand up. That we should look to Africa from where
shall come our hope and our deliverance. And so, him they
betrayed. They called him a next Bedward and say that he
was mad.
And Howell did build Pinnacle in Jamaica, and he say that
we should grow we own food. And soon they drive him too,
from jail to madhouse because they can't deal with what he
talking. And so the people just scatter like sand. Some of we

run to Costa Rica, some of we run to Panama. Some to The
States. Some to England to follow Garvey.

When you say Pocomania, the government don't mind, it all
right. When you say Cumina, they no mind. But when you
say RASTA? It's pure jail and madhouse them have for you.
So me, I come Brooklyn, bake me bread in morning time
and keep meself well quiet. Stay from out the people them
way. Me just read me Bible and I watch and wait. When I
see Lindsay he just make me sad because he a dreamer
and I know what they have for him. *(Makes a snapping
motion with his fingers meaning LICKS).* When I was a
child I spake as a child
I thought as a child,
But then I came a man *(Pause)* and I became afraid . . .

Darkness

SCENE X
STUDY FOR WEST INDIAN FUNERAL

*Full cast of actors playing mourners at funeral. The women all wear
the dark coats of old and over-dressed women. The men wear suits
and white gloves and carry the society banners such as they do for
the death of a member. The Minister, Reverend Girtey, is weary with
age and walks with cane.*

WOMEN *(Singing)*
>Oh Lamb of God
>Oh Lamb of God
>Oh Lamb of God that taketh away the sins of the world
>Grant us thy peace.

REVEREND   Where is my text now? *(Searching until he finds it)*
>We ask you Lord to take unto your bosom the soul of the
>departed Harold Murray, a Chef by profession and a
>Mason. We all remember him as a faithful husband to Anne
>Murray, and a loyal member of the St. Andrew's parish.

Although he did not always attend church services, he never failed in his commitment. He always sent in his gleaner every year and contributed to the church organ.

WOMAN   *(Whispering to her friend)* Organ? I hear him talking about organ, organ, five years now and I don't see no organ still.

REVEREND   *(Adjusting glasses and continues)* Which with the grace of God we should have before too long, into the arms of Abraham we offer his spirit . . . Amen.

CHORUS   Amen.

Darkness

The scene is before an open coffin. The family members standing about. The last remaining son is named, Clayton. He walks before the casket and looks inside to study the body for a moment. He is only about 37 but looks 15 years older.

CLAYTON   Well father, you always said that if I didn't bury you right you were going come back and strangle me in me sleep. *(Pause)* Okay, here you go. Spent $1,200 on your casket. So you should feel real good.

Right about now the others of the family begin to suspect that Clayton might be drunk and begin to get nervous.

CLAYTON   Yes indeed, Papa Murray, finally laid down. *(Pause)* Well I just want a chance to say that I think you were about the most cruel bastard I ever met in my life. You destroyed three of your children.

MOTHER   Clayton! What's wrong with you? You don't have to do this here.

CLAYTON   No, you know how long I waited for this. *(Turns back to coffin)* You destroyed all three of your children. He killed his first wife, my mother, he worked her to death. And was doing good at damn near working his second wife to death. *(Turns and looks at his step-mother)*

MINISTER   *(Trying to take him by the arm)* This is not the place.

CLAYTON   Leave me alone. All I'm talking here tonight is truth. He brought me here from the islands when I was five. And all the kids in Harlem and The Bronx used to make fun of me because I had an accent so bad that I developed a stammer and this son of a bitch used to always tell me I was a dummy because of it.

MINISTER   Clayton!

CLAYTON   Then when I was 12 years old my sister Carol died, she was 18 and he turned to me and said why did God take her, why not you or your brother Peter? She was the only one that had brains in the family. Yeah, he said that to me. He surely did. Then when I started getting interested in painting, like when I was 15, he comes along and throws all my paints and stuff out the window 'cause he's talking about he don't want me be no sissy. He want me to get a job like he did back home when he was my age. You know I had to hear all of that every damn day?

MOTHER   Clayton, you can't do this here, son.

CLAYTON   And when I was 17, I went off to the army to get away from this bastard. And then they shipped me to Vietnam, them crackers there were worse than you. They wanted to send me to the front line so I can get my ass killed. Yeah, they were sending all us young niggers to the front line. Meanwhile they lay back and gave orders, all them red necks. *(Pause)* And when I cracked up and they had to discharge me to the hospital, all this man here had to say *(pointing to the coffin)* was 'You always was weak.' *(Pause)* By the time I was 21, my brother Peter had done killed himself. And I was an alcoholic. See what I mean. *(Looking into the coffin)* That was your gift to me, nigger.

Mother starts to cry.

CLAYTON   But it's all right. All I know is, that if there is a Hell,

then I know where you going. For the Hell you made of
everybody's life. Good West Indian father. Cruel like a bull,
and just as spiteful as a dog. *(Long pause)* And what you
never knew was that out of three of us, I was the only one
who ever really loved you. *(Exits)*

The other members of the funeral gossip.

SCENE XI
WEST INDIAN BOATRIDE – LABOR DAY IN NEW YORK

Chorus spinning, dancing hard calypso

VOICE   Victoria boatride boy. Hold that tiger. *(Arms extended over
his head, sweat dripping off him)*

LINDSAY   *(Standing and watching)* Why you drink so much Ellis?
Why you belly so fat?

ELLIS   I drink to work man. I work hard, you know.

LINDSAY   *(Speaking to the woman Ellis is dancing with)* Kate why
you eat so, you don't need all that food, girl?

KATE   I does like to eat. I could eat your portion and my portion
and still go back again. When I come home from me work,
I tired. I eat and fall into my bed.

LINDSAY   Why you so nervous all the time, Ellis?

ELLIS   I not nervous, I happy.

LINDSAY   You not happy.

ELLIS   Don't tell me I not happy. I kill you. Don't tell me I not
happy I chop off your damn neck. *(The others restrain him)*

Enter Iantha and Wilfred. The man is very effete.

IANTHA   I tried of this bati-man I with, his mother make a
woman of him. I'm married to a woman. I married to a

bati-man. *(The man slaps her.)*

LINDSAY Come on my sister.

GIRL Where you want to take me?

LINDSAY This boat sinking.

GIRL I can't go from here, that's me people them.

LINDSAY Boat sinking girl.

GIRL My parents and you ask me to leave them? And over there is my sister who has my face.

LINDSAY They have you face but not you soul. Boat sinking fast.

He extends his hands and they touch. Music builds to darkness.

Darkness

SCENE XII
BEGGAR BO BARRETT IN NIGHT TOWN

The entrance is again night. After twelve. The hour when the duppies (Zombies) walk the islands. But we are in New York now, a place called Brooklyn and the zombies which walk here are quite different from those of the islands.

Beggar Bo is older now, the skin does not look as blessed with the sun. It is now the face of a man who has been indoors for a long period of time. The lighting is that of a bar. The scene starts with a solitary figure bending over a glass. The bar keeper comes over to his table and begins to pick up glass. Bo quickly stops him.

BEGGAR BO   That's cool man, rest. I still drinking.

BAR KEEPER   Thought that glass was empty.

BEGGAR BO   Still a corner here man. Rum expensive here man,
you'll tief too bad. *(Bar keeper goes off angry)* They funny,
not even here a year self good, already them don't know
you no more. Sometimes me does have to ask: Brother,
don't you remember when we did run the bush together.
When we was just two pickney, and when our shoes would
have holes in them as if they laughing. We use to stick
newspaper inside for sole.

You don't remember? *(Approaches startled girl)*

Sister? Do you remember many times we use to rub our
bodies up. You and me. It's a long time I know you. I
remember when you was so poor you stick toilet paper for
you bombo cloth. But that's all gone. Now you here in
America and you big time nurse and you can't talk to
Beggar Bo now. You all leave you two and three pickney
them in rass bush and now you is a virgin again, and butter
melt in you mouth 'Miss Too Nice'.
But it cool though, you know, Beggar Bo not talking. *(He
laughs)* We leave where the people them poor and all bend
up like copper wire. I glad you doing good. But Lord you
all memory is short. The woman come here to this country
and them turn cruel like beast. Them faces hard like man,
them bodies get fat and all them want do is make money
and sleep. Some of these woman look so much like witch
that all them does need is broomstick. *(Pause)* Yes man,
woman turn beast here in this place. These people strange.

(Stage lit only with lanterns)

BEGGAR BO   So dearly did God love the world that He sent His
only begotton son to be sacrificed for the sins of man. There
was a man whose name was John, he was not the Light but
was sent to bear witness of that Light. He came unto his
own and his own received him not.

(Someone throws him a coin)

. . . I say he came unto his own and his own received him
not, but *(bends to pick up several coins)* as many as
received him, to them gave he power. *(Counts money)* . . .
Well Lord, I see you not through a glass darkly, but face to
face. I'm here in the United States, here among the most
asleep of the asleep. I should be happy I suppose. I seen
men so poor that when they shit nothing comes out but
their soul. Lindsay, when we were young we knew there
was nothing bigger than us. There was no man we 'fraid, no
mind brighter than our own. But we men now and the
world is a little harder than that *(smiling)* ain't it?

(Turns his back to audience then urinates)

I make a little pee pee to help the earth grow . . . You know
sometimes I does have a mind to die, and sometimes I
does want to live forever. You know how you does feel so
bad sometimes when you see so much suffering. You see
people running behind they shadows *(simply)* and they
never going to catch it. You does feel bad sometimes, they
so lost.

CHORUS   *(Nodding in agreement)* Yes Beggar Bo!

BEGGAR BO   *(Walks along suddenly caught up in reverie, again
addressing Lindsay)* And remember Lindsay, how my aunt
would tell us to be careful for lizard and snake in the fields.
And we walk along all day looking for snake and no
snakes come. *(Pause)* And when I first come into the city,
they ask me who I was and who's son and I say I Charles
Wade son, and me people them is Bramble. And me
grandmother, one Mistress Frances, who live on Corkhill.
They came forward to me and their hands were open. And
the night come down so soft, soft and me feel so good I
want to put me hand on it, the night feel so good *(Pause,
new breath)* Remember, was the Carnival. Fireworks make
flowers of light, and we was so scared we jump into bed

because jumbie men would get us and they was seven feet tall on they stilts and they eyes red as fire, pass the space of window. *(Pause)* And now is night, and all the harm man can do himself for today is done. And it's night now. Even God my Father going to forgive me when the sky get black with birds. (*Moves the following line like a prayer*) I in America now Lindsay. This lump of idleness. And I waiting so long. But I gone play a tune so sweet so sweet that even God will forgive me home.

The old women of the chorus scream: 'Go on, Beggar Bo'

FIRST CHORUS WOMAN   *(Carrying her lantern in her hand as she exits. Her touch on him ends the ritual)* You does dream nice Beggar Bo.

SECOND CHORUS WOMAN   *(Following)* He does dream nice yes.

FIRST CHORUS WOMAN   You know I does have a pain here *(rubs shoulder)* in me shoulder when night come. It hurt me bad, man.

SECOND CHORUS WOMAN   You should rub with some Liamcol.

SCENE XIII
RITUAL

Lindsay, the nephew, now transformed to the Juju man. The keeper of the chalice and the scribe of his race. The ritual has come full circuit. The scene is Woodlawn Cemetry in New York, where so many West Indians have been laid to rest with a century. The stage is lit by candle.

JUJU MAN   You in the graveyard now, Uncle Harold. You in the graveyard now.

CHORUS   Burn the candle

Burn the candle
When the one shall be two

JUJU MAN   And death shall have no dominion and the earth
shall give up her dead. By the waters of Babylon there I sat
down.

CHORUS   Burn the candle. Come join the jamboree.

JUJU MAN   The Lord is my shepherd I shall not want for anything. You hear me? For anything. He maketh me to lie
down beside the still waters. When I tired and I find myself
weary as Jesus, he restoreth my soul he prepareth a table
before me in the presence of my enemies. Right before
them who wish me dead, and my very cup runneth over.
(Laughing) But I going to burn down Babylon, get out me
way I have wings. *(Spinning)* Is you own greed going do
you in.

CHORUS   Armegeddon. Call the tribes.

JUJU MAN   I calling. This for you, my uncle. I waking you, uncle.
Walking you through Egypt land. The thirtieth hour. Give
them music to walk

Music builds

I calling
I calling Montserrat
I calling Antigua
I calling Aruba
I calling one Guyana, one Guyana
I calling Nevis
I calling Panama
I calling Surinam
I calling St. Lucia
I calling St. Kitts
I calling St. Vincent
I calling the Exumas
Martinique I calling
Barbados where they broke us

Trinidad where they take us
Dominica where the breed us
Haiti where they work us
Grenada where they whip us
I calling Jah Obeah
I calling Jah Obeah . . .

Slow darkness . . . curtain

LIKE THEM THAT DREAM
(Children of Ogun)

CHARACTERS

SPARROW .... A young South African painter
SHARON .... A young Black American in her Twenties
VAN MUELLIN A retired member of the South African secret service
MISS DERRIS .... A nurse

SETTING
New York City, (Greenwich Village, Riverside Drive)

TIME
The present

ACT 1

SCENE 1

*Sparrow enters stage carrying a large sketch pad under one arm
and a folding chair in the other. He also carries a mysterious
umbrella. He is just about to start his day as a street painter. He is in
his thirties and has an enigmatic smile which escapes from the
blackness of his face. He very carefully chooses his spot and then,
deciding that everything is perfect, begins his invocation.*

SPARROW   The Lord is my light and my salvation whom shall I
fear?
(He exclaims:) AY! I YO! The Lord is the very strength of
my life *(He laughs)* of whom shall I be afraid?
When the wicked, even my enemies and my foes, came
upon me *(Pause)*
To eat up my flesh,
They stumbled and fell.
(Laughs again and looks about him)
New York, New York, city of miracles.
Are you the new Jerusalem in the desert?
Don't I say!
Your son is a long way from Jo'burg now mother.
A long way from your city of gold and blood.
(Slaps his hands together)
Today I am going to paint a thousand women. I'll paint
their eyes and their voices, and carve smiles out of the
darkness of their faces.

*He chooses someone in the audience to communicate with
throughout the play. This person he calls NKOSI.*

You don't believe me Nkosi? Watch me good and see if I
lie.

He turns back to his sketch pad – a woman passes.

SPARROW   My Lord, My Lord what a woman
(He bends down to see better then stands again)
But no, it can't be. Girl, you are beautiful.
(Girl looks at him gives him an undecided response)
Forgive me, I know that it is not done that way here. Let me
start again, I would like to paint you if you would let me.

GIRL   I don't really have the time now . . .

SPARROW   Please, its important.

GIRL   Why is it important?

SPARROW   Because I want to paint you – now.

GIRL   So?

SPARROW   Are you afraid of me?

GIRL   No, I'm not afraid.

SPARROW   Then why?

GIRL   I'm sort of busy, you see, time . . .

SPARROW   What is time to the day? It means so little and even
less to the night.

GIRL   *(After a pause)* All right, I'll go for it, but if it don't look like
me, I'm not buying.

SPARROW   Beautiful, sit, please. *(Starts on sketch)*

GIRL   Anyway you going give this to me right?

SPARROW   *Starts to hum South African song*

GIRL   Is there anyway you want me to pose?

SPARROW   No, I don't want you to pose. But I want you to think
of something.

GIRL   What?

SPARROW   Think about, if we had to meet in secret. If everywhere
was police. You must think about them watching every

movement and every thought which passes between us.
(The girl gets frightened) Your eyes are the difference
between the way the world should be and the way it really
is. *(He starts to paint)*

Darkness

SCENE II

*Sparrow in winter. He is wrapped in a jacket and scarf. The grim-
ness of a New York winter settles about him. He is in the same location in the village neat the 8th Avenue subway stop.*

SPARROW   *(Addressing audience)* You know, Nkosi, when I was
twenty my father decided it was time that I started the long
journey. He wanted me to go abroad and study. He wanted
me to take degree in Economics and Sociology like
Nkrumah. But I had other plans.

(He stands up as if addressing father)

My father, I would like to speak with you.
'Is it heavy my son?'
Yes father, it is heavy.
You say you would like for me to go to England to study.
You say you want me to be a teacher. But you see father, I
do not wish to be a teacher. I want to be an artist, a painter.

(Pause)

'What did you say my son, I didn't hear you. I could not
have heard you right. It sounded as if you said you did not
wish to be a teacher.' No father, I do not want to teach, I
want to paint. Paint our soul, paint our dreams.

(Sudden lightning movement like three slaps)

Wham! Wham! Wham!
Nkosi, I couldn't tell you if the earth came up to me or I
went down to it. All I can remember is trying to get up from

off the kitchen floor and all these stars running around in
my brain.

'You want to be a what, a painter like those boys in the street
those outee boys who the police chase. Is this why I work
like a beast in the mines? Is this why your mother work as a
domestic carrying white women's piss pots?'

And so, there was no further argument.

Nkosi, I left the white man's South Africa and went to the
white man's England *(Pause)* to study. Sociology and
Economics like Nkrumah, like Nyerere. But I found few
English men, Nkosi. they were mostly South Africans,
Rhodesians, White Kenyans. Those who can steal, steal.
Those who can't, teach.

They said that England was a nation of shop keepers but
now half the shops were shut and what they sold was not
bread but arms. Arms for war. They smiled with British
smiles and read their London Times.

I came trying to escape South Africa but they followed me.
They follow me Nkosi, like a ghost dripping my blood.

(Pause)

And so I tried America.

New York in winter, Nkosi. Different mood now. Just a
greyness and the winter stops the hands of painters. Eh,
what I say. Even the rats hide from the streets.

But I don't fear you New York, not me Nkosi. This is no
winter. This is a child winter. You want big winter you must
come Jo'burg. You must come Egoli: In South Africa that is
winter. When babies die. When they leave the womb.
(Makes a movement of a child being born) When they jump
out into the world and they see the scene and feel the lash
of cold. They say no mother, you will not trap me so. Better
to go back where I come from. Better the darkness of the
mines. They say inside you mother was summer but outside
you is winter. Better dead. Better dead. So what are you to
me New York, I can only laugh at your winter. *(sees
Sharon)*

But wait Nkosi, I know that girl.

(Approaches her she is well dressed in boots and sensible coat)

Hello my sister.

SHARON   What? Oh, it's you.

SPARROW   Yes the painter, you remember. You never came back for your sketch.

SHARON   I've been busy. I go to night school now twice a week.

SPARROW   Night school, that's good, very good.

SHARON   What have you been doing?

SPARROW   *(Opens his hands in a gesture)* Surviving all this.

SHARON   All what?

SPARROW   The world my sister, the world.

SHARON   Are you painting still?

SPARROW   Must paint.

SHARON   Well it doesn't look like the best time for painting in the street. Hey, aren't you cold?

SPARROW   Cold me? Oh no, can't be cold. This is A-MER-I-CA. The land of opportunity. No cold in America.

SHARON   Oh yeah. Well more power to you. You keep on believing that. Look I've got to be getting home. I'll see you around.

SPARROW   *(As she starts to go he follows her)* Listen, I have that sketch for you. I finished it.

SHARON   Oh yeah, that's nice, well you hold on to it.

SPARROW   It's really beautiful.

SHARON   Well I hope you can sell it. *(She starts to leave again.)*

SPARROW   *(Outraged)* Sell it? Sell it. I would never sell it. Do you think that everything in this world lives and dies with the dollar. Some men carry their soul like a brief case. They put it down here, they put it down there.

SHARON   Wow, listen it's no big thing, I just thought you could use a bit of money. I mean I don't mind if you sell it.

SPARROW   I would mind.

SHARON   Well then don't sell it, you know, if that's how you feel. *(Turns to go again)*

SPARROW   *(Gravely)* That's how I feel.

SHARON   No big thing, bye.

SPARROW   It is a big thing. A very big thing.

> *She notices he no longer tries to stop her. She then stops and turns*

SHARON   Why?

SPARROW   Why what?

SHARON   Why is it a big thing?

SPARROW   Because I care, Sharon.

SHARON   How come you remember my name?

SPARROW   Because it's very important to me, my sister.

SHARON   A lot of things seem to be important to you.

SPARROW   Everything is important to me that has to do with you.

SHARON   Why?

SPARROW   Because whas has to do with you, has to do with me.

SHARON   How can you say that? You don't even know me.

SPARROW   I know you.

SHARON   *(Defiant)* You don't know me!

SPARROW   I don't know you.

SHARON   How you know me?

SPARROW   It would take time to tell you.

SHARON   What am I doing standing talking with you? Its cold out
here. I got to go home.

SPARROW   Because here in this city of cities
Where nothing is any big thing,
We passed like them that dream
but we come together again.
Do you understand now?

SHARON   *(Pause)* No.

SPARROW   What I'm trying to say is that since I last saw you I've
seen a lot of nothing. And you have seen a lot of nothing
and now we see each other again.

SHARON   You got some rap, talk more shit than the radio.
(Touches his jacket) Ain't you cold?

SPARROW   I told you this is . . .

SHARON   I know, I know, America land of opportunity.

SPARROW   Can't be cold here, my sister.

SHARON   You keep believing that and your behind catch
pneumonia.

SPARROW   Would you take care of me if I caught the
pneumonia?

SHARON   Listen, I work in the hospital but I ain't no nurse, I'm a
technician. If you get sick I can't help you.

SPARROW   Would you like something to drink?

SHARON   I'm not much of a drinker.

SPARROW   Me too.

SHARON   Me too what?

SPARROW   Not much of a drinker.

SHARON   I got to be going. So when am I going see this big time
       sketch?

SPARROW   Tonight.

SHARON   Tonight?

SPARROW   I'll show it to you now.

SHARON   You live around here.

SPARROW   Yes my sister, all around here.

SHARON   Well I can't stop now, I have to be . . .

SPARROW   Getting home.

SHARON   That's right. *(Pause)* You're making fun of me. You
       think I'm crazy. Well I think you're crazy.

SPARROW   No. No.
       They walk along together

SHARON   Nigger, why you don't wear a coat. You Africans hot
       blooded or something? I'm freezing.

SPARROW   Can you cook?

SHARON   Not too good.

SPARROW   I'll teach you.

SHARON   You'll teach me, when?

SPARROW   At your house, while I show you the sketch. Come.
       (He leads her)

SHARON   Say what . . .

       Darkness

SCENE III

Sharon's house on Riverside Drive. They enter her apartment

SHARON   I don't usually let men into my apartment when I just meet them.

SPARROW   Me too.

SHARON   Me too what?

SPARROW   Don't let just-meet men into my apartment.

SHARON   Well this is it.

> *Sparrow enters very deliberately as though choosing an area to set up his easel. Finds right spot and sits on floor.*

SHARON   What's that, your spot?

SPARROW   Yes.

SHARON   So what's your name! Sparrow?

SPARROW   That's right.

SHARON   I mean what's your real name?

SPARROW   Is so.

SHARON   I mean your full name.

SPARROW   Mr. Sparrow.

SHARON   You want to look at television?

SPARROW   No.

SHARON   You don't *(Unbelieving)*

SPARROW   Oh sorry. Yes, yes, I love to see television.

SHARON   That's all right, you don't have to. You want to hear some music.

SPARROW   Nice.

SHARON   So where you live, in the Village? *(Puts on record)*

SPARROW No.

SHARON Where you live?

SPARROW I don't.

SHARON You don't what?

SPARROW Live.

SHARON So your name is Sparrow and you don't live anywhere?

SPARROW Yes.

SHARON *(Taking off record)* Well listen, I got to get up kind of early tomorrow so I'm going to have to make this an early night.

SPARROW Here! *(takes out sketch pad and suddenly shows her the sketch of herself)*

SHARON Well, I'll be damn, you really did do a sketch. I thought you were lying, It's nice I mean it's good. May I look at the rest of these?

SPARROW Yes.

SHARON *(Looking through pad)* These are all right Sparrow. Why do you just sketch in the street? I mean you could do this serious.

SPARROW *(Laughing)* Serious?

SHARON You know what I mean. You so weird. *(Looks at work and then at him)* I used to do some drawing when I was in High School.

SPARROW I know.

SHARON How you know. Oh, you know everything, right?

SPARROW Not everything, my sister.

SHARON And stop calling me your sister. And I thought you was going cook me this dinner, Mr. Chef?

SPARROW   Oh yes *(He gets up)* You show me the kitchen.

SHARON   You not going take off your jacket and scarf?

SPARROW   I never take this off.

SHARON   Never?

SPARROW   Where your man, Sharon?

SHARON   Why, what you want to know for? Listen, I'm just
getting over someone, right, so I don't want to get involved,
okay?

SPARROW   Right. What food you have?

SHARON   Chicken. Sorry, no steak.

SPARROW   Chicken and rice. Paradise. Truly my redeemer liveth.

SHARON   Your redeemer what?

SPARROW   Liveth, liveth Sharon, liveth.

   Darkness

SCENE IV

*After dinner. Sharon sucking on a chicken bone. Sparrow seated on
floor with plate on lap.*

SHARON   That was nice. You really can cook.

SPARROW   Lift up your heads, oh ye gates
Even lift them up, ye everlasting doors.

SHARON   What are you, a preacher?

SPARROW   Church school, Sharon, church school. They make us
sing all the hymns in South Africa, good christian country.
Lot of hymns and bible class and no peeking under girls
dresses either. A lot of 'forgive me father for I have sinned'
and no Playboy Magazines. A good country, don't I say.

SHARON   South Africa?

SPARROW   Yes, yes, my sister.

SHARON   But don't they have apartheid and beating niggers over the head and shooting and carrying on?

SPARROW   Like I say, a good Christian country.

SHARON   But I thought – oh well – just like in the South over here I guess. South is South. *(She takes the plates)* Are you glad to be here Sparrow? *(She exits off stage with dishes)*

SPARROW   Yes the apartment is nice and warm.

SHARON   *(Returns)* I mean here in America.

SPARROW   Oh America, of youth, great great don't I say land of . . .

SHARON   Yeah, yeah, are you ever serious?

SPARROW   Always serious Sharon, always. Tell me, why do you cover your mouth with your hand when you eat?

SHARON   I don't know habit I guess. My mother does it. Why?

SPARROW   My mother does it too and my sister. As if the food is stolen.

SHARON   I never thought about it. You notice everything don't you? *(Shakes her head)* You're weird you know that. So tell me about these bible classes. What did they teach you?

SPARROW   Afrikaans.

SHARON   What's that, a language?

SPARROW   More than a language Sharon, a religion.

SHARON   And they taught you the Ten Commandments? *(She begins to leaf through sketch pad again)*

SPARROW   More than ten Sharon. they taught us the ten "thou shalt nots" and then two more.

SHARON   Two more?

SPARROW   'Thou shalt not get caught because thou shalt be
killed.' And 'Thou shalt not want because thou shalt
not have.'

SHARON   Damn, I don't know how you all take it.

SPARROW   One day at a time.

SHARON   I guess so.

SPARROW   But I don't want to talk about Johannesburg, I don't
want to talk about Capetown. I don't want to talk about
Soweto. I want to talk about God and how He made you.

SHARON   What?

SPARROW   I want to talk about how He made your breast go up
so. And your round ass and the things He did with your
eyes.

SHARON   I hear you . . . um . . . (Nervous) . . . Its getting late, listen
I think that . . .(He holds her in a way she can't move) You
too much . . . (He kisses her)
Listen I don't want to get . . . (He kisses her) involved.

SPARROW   Me too.

   Darkness

SCENE V

Three months later, Sharon's apartment.

SPARROW   Women are funny, Nkosi. they like to test you at first.
They leave purses full of money about the apartment. They
tell you help yourself. They don't count the change (Pause)
right away! They wait.
The first month when you move in they call a few times a
day to make sure you haven't escaped.

The first month is always good, Nkosi. You want it steady every night. You get mad when she is having her period. Soon you learn that this is a little gift from God. It gives man a chance to think for a week.

(Stops and looks up) Thank you my God, how wise you are. I don't go out much, Nkosi, I'm trying to pass through the exile of winter. Faces outside look so grim. It's nice to have a little woman going out every morning to work. You have to admire them.

Sits on floor crosses legs and turns on television with the sound off.

God bless woman. God bless America. God bless work.

Sharon enters house.

Funny though, Nkosi, lately she's been giving me strange looks.

Sharon puts down bag of groceries and stares at him, turns away and gives him second look again.

I think I feel a breeze. *(Turns to her)*

Hello Sharon.

SHARON   Well I see you had a nice day.

SPARROW   Eh, no kiss kiss no more? Tell me about everything at work today. You must tell me everything. You must leave nothing out.

SHARON   I'm tired, they work my ass today. What you been doing? Oh I see the usual. In front of the television. Why don't you turn the sound if you going look at it?

SPARROW   No need for sound, I can read their lips. They have nothing to tell me anyway.

SHARON   If they have nothing to tell you why don't you turn it off?

SPARROW   Can't turn it off, this is America.

SHARON   Listen Sparrow, we going to have to have a little talk.
   (Turns off television)

SPARROW   Eh, you turned it off.

SHARON   This nigger is crazy. Look, don't you think it's time you
   tried to do something.

SPARROW   Do something?

SHARON   You know, like, work.

SPARROW   Oh, work.

SHARON   Yeah work, you know that word?

SPARROW   You mean *their* work. I already do my work.

SHARON   Yeah well your work not bringing in no money, you
   know what I mean.

   He falls on floor in melodramatic motion.

   Look I like your work very much believe me, but . . . Don't
   you ever want your own money?

SPARROW   No.

SHARON   I guess not, as long as . . .

SPARROW   Say it, long as I have yours.

(He leaps up grabs his jacket and his sketch pads)

SHARON   *(Holds him)* Wait a minute. God, you're so sensitive. I
   didn't say you should leave, I'm not kicking you out.

SPARROW   Where should I work? I mean of course I should work
   if I could. My father's son is not lazy *(Watches her from the
   corner of his eye)* But there is nothing.

SHARON   Oh, they have one or two jobs going at the hospital, I
   asked for you.

SPARROW   Oh . . . that was good of you.

SHARON   You say you need supplies.

SPARROW   Yes I need things.

SHARON   Well you didn't think that I . . .

SPARROW   Oh no, of course not.

SHARON   So are you going to for for the interview.

SPARROW   What is for, brain surgeon?

SHARON   You'll have to make do with orderly or nurse's aide.

SPARROW   Oh.

SHARON   What's the matter, why you look so sad?

SPARROW   I had wanted brain surgeon.

SHARON   *(Taking his sketch pad and things from out of his hands and slowly undressing him)* Well, maybe next time honey.

Darkness

ACT II

SCENE 1

The Hospital

SPARROW   You know Nkosi this life is a funny thing. A funny
thing is life, Nkosi. You never know a damn thing except
that you don't know. Life is like a jealous man who
guards his woman from all other men's eyes and then one
day on his death bed he finds that she was really a lesbian all
along.
(Mimes shock)
Where can one hide from life, Nkosi? Now look at me, pos
(a curse word, lights a cigarette).
Back home we had fights every week. Knife fight, bottle
fight, rock fight, any excuse. Of course it was all right
because it was only black man killing black man. They
never mind that. Anyhow I spend a lot of time in hospital,
there's not a part of my body which has not break, *(Pause)*
broke. *(Thinks)* Yes broke. I never thought I would work in a
hospital but then you never quite know do you Nkosi,
which way this life will go.
(Looks about him)
Oh this is a nice hospital. A white man's hospital. No smell
of death. No bodies lined up in the hall ways. This is a
good time hospital different to Soweto.
I wouldn't mind having my skull cracked here. Would even
be fun. In South Africa they steal black men's hearts for
transplant surgery. I remember one Saturday night back
home. You see there was this girl, Jean, beautiful girl, what
a woman. I met her at this party and . . .

*Behind him the supervisor Miss Derris, an Irish nurse calls
him for his interview. The light comes up on her.*

MISS DERRIS   Mr. Sparrow?

SPARROW   Oh sorry Nkosi, I'll come back just now. *(Turns to Miss Derris)* Yes, Sparrow here.

Meticulously puts out cigarette and puts it behind his ear to smoke later.

MISS DERRIS   Sit down please. I'm Miss Derris. Have you filled out your form?

SPARROW   Yes, Miss.

MISS DERRIS   Sparrow, is that your first name or surname?

SPARROW   Eh, surname, Miss.

MISS DERRIS   And what is your first name?

SPARROW   Ti.

MISS DERRIS   T?

SPARROW   Yes. T-i.

MISS DERRIS   Oh, as in tie.

SPARROW   Yes. I have another name. Naphtali but that comes from God and only my mother calls it.

MISS DERRIS   I see, have you ever worked in a hospital before?

SPARROW   Oh yes, I've spent a lot of time in hospitals.

MISS DERRIS   As a technician?

SPARROW   No, but very technical.

MISS DERRIS   As an orderly?

SPARROW   Yes.

MISS DERRIS   Well we need someone to take the patients back and forth to the operating room and to get X-rays.

SPARROW   Oh, no problem.

MISS DERRIS   What is this, address here you gave? *(Trying to read)*

SPARROW   Oh, 475 The Drive of River.

MISS DERRIS   The Drive of River . . . You mean Riverside Drive.

SPARROW   Oh yes . . . sorry.

MISS DERRIS   Sharon has recommended you very strongly. She's
    a very nice girl.

SPARROW   Oh yes.

MISS DERRIS   Where are you from?

SPARROW   South Africa.

MISS DERRIS   You've come a long way, haven't you?

SPARROW   Oh yes a very long way.

MISS DERRIS   Well, I too have come a long way. I'm from Ireland,
    have you heard of Ireland?

SPARROW   Part of England.

MISS DERRIS   Well they like to think so. We don't. Are all your
    papers in order?

SPARROW   Oh yes.

MISS DERRIS   Well we'll give you an chance and see how you
    work out. Can you start Monday? Don't be late.

SPARROW   Hey don't I say. No mos late.

MISS DERRIS   What?

SPARROW   I mean thank you Miss D.

    Darkness

SCENE II

On the Hospital ward. Sparrow carries an orderly's uniform.

SPARROW   Hey Nkosi, I'm a worker you know. Hey mos worker.

What more a man could want? In America land of the opportunity. Muck me! Back home a Juba would kill his mother for a chance to be here. A job, a steady goose, in this time of new government and big time deals in Washington.

(Like a school boy)

Truly I am delivered.

(Dressing into hospital orderly uniform)

Funny how nice women are to you when they know you're working. They give you that little extra at night *(Mimes sign of copulation)* and feed you double portion at dinner. Ja, so this world goes.

(Fully dressed now)

Go see what my girl is doing.

Light comes up on Sharon who is working over a microscope in a laboratory.

(He goes up to her and grabs her about the waist) Hey bokkie, how is it?

SHARON   You scared me. What are you doing here? Shouldn't you be upstairs on the ward?

SPARROW   All quiet there. I just come to see what time you going for lunch. They let you eat, don't they?

SHARON   I'll take lunch about one.

SPARROW   I'll come for you.

SHARON   How's it going?

SPARROW   Nice. My kind of job; nothing to do. Just stay out of their way.

SHARON   You better be careful. Go back before they miss you.

SPARROW   Don't worry, bokkie. Hey listen I found an empty

room, 846, we could spend some time, you know. Don't I
say.

SHARON   You're crazy. Can't you wait until tonight? Anyhow I've
got work to do.

SPARROW   Okay, I'm gone *(Kisses her)*

SHARON   Sparrow try not to get fired, will you?

SPARROW   Okay okay, stop worrying.

Darkness

SCENE III

Back on the ward

SPARROW   I'll tell you, Nkosi, nothing like working in a hospital
to make you want a woman. Maybe its because of the death
that's all around you. You are so glad for the little piece of
life that's moving between your legs. One thing I know,
Nkosi, Hell is to get old and have to die here among these
people and their mercy.
I saw a nurse force a pair of false teeth in an old woman's
mouth. They weren't even her teeth.
Let me die. Better to die among those you know, than to
have to live like this among strangers.
Some of these white people are funny. They live on out of
spite. The husband wants to live to see the wife dead. The
wife won't go before the husband and so they hang on by
their fingernails. Hey, what a life.

An old white man suddenly appears in his wheelchair.

MAN   *(Wheeling himself about menacingly)* Nurse, Nurse!

SPARROW   Can I help you?

MAN   Not you Kaffir, I want the nurse. You robbed me.

SPARROW   I what?

MAN   You robbed me. I had ten dollars under my mattress and it's gone. I want the nurse in charge.

SPARROW   I didn't rob you. I've never seen you before.

MAN   Are you calling me a liar? Are you saying I didn't have my money there?

SPARROW   I don't know anything about your money.

MAN   God, die BLIKSEM KAFFIR IS BEDONNERD. Nurse!

SPARROW   You dirty Boer, stinking Boer bastard.

MAN   Where you from?

SPARROW   The same place you're from.

MAN   A Bantu Kaffir Ja? Alright, Jong, you'll pay for this. Nurse!

   Miss Derris enters.

MISS DERRIS   What's going on here?

·MAN   He robbed me.

SPARROW   He's a liar.

MISS DERRIS   How did he rob you?

MAN   He stole money from my room while I was asleep.

SPARROW   I've never been in his room.

MISS DERRIS   Did you see him enter your room, Mr. Van Muellin?

SPARROW   Van Muellin? *(Stares at man)*

MAN   I tell you I was asleep, how could I see him?

MISS DERRIS   Then you have no right to accuse him.

MAN   He's a Bantu from the homelands. I don't want him working here.

MISS DERRIS   You have no right to say who can work here and
who can't, Mr. Van Muellin. This is not South Africa.

MAN   You don't have to tell me, I know it's not South Africa.
That's why this place is such a mess. You just see to it this
Kaffir stays away from my room, Ja?

MISS DERRIS   You pay no mind to him.

SPARROW   Van Muellin.

Darkness

SCENE IV

Late that night. Sparrow enters Sharon's apartment

SHARON   Sparrow?

SPARROW   Yes it's me.

SHARON   Where the hell have you been?

SPARROW   Walking, just walking.

SHARON   Until three in the morning.

SPARROW   I had to think, okay?

SHARON   Think? Is that what your doing? *(Turns on the light)* Let
me look at you. Come here. You've been drinking.

SPARROW   Yeah so.

SHARON   Take off your shirt. *(She starts to take off his shirt)*

SPARROW   What you look for?

SHARON   Nothing just let me see.

SPARROW   Christ, this isn't South Africa. I don't have to strip.
(He jumps up)

SHARON   It's not that I don't believe you Sparrow, it's just that . . .

SPARROW   You don't believe me.

SHARON   Right.

SPARROW   What do you expect to find?

SHARON   Well when a man suddenly disappears and doesn't come home until three in the morning, you got to admit it's kind of strange. Its makes a girl kind of feel like maybe he's using her for a fool, you know what I mean?

SPARROW   Where do you think I've been?

SHARON   I wouldn't know. You ought to know better than me.

SPARROW   I haven't been with any other girl.

SHARON   Then let me see your back.

He lifts up shirt for inspection and bends over, drops trousers.

So what was it you had to think about?

SPARROW   Van Muellin.

SHARON   Van what . . . did you catch something?

SPARROW   Sharon, Van Muellin is a South African. He was in the Secret Service in South Africa. He was in charge of interrogation. He changed his name from Von Mellenthin.

SHARON   So?

SPARROW   So, he happens to be a patient in the hospital.

SHARON   Does he know you?

SPARROW   He doesn't know me from back home but I know him. When I was a student we held protest rallies. My cousin Cepo was taken for questioning. He was never seen again. They say he just disappeared.

SHARON   Disappeared?

SPARROW   Many people disappear back home, girl. Disappearing is a way of life. But it was Van Muellin who was in charge. Van Muellin always got the information he wanted. He would tell you when you entered, 'You can make it easy or you can make it hard, you can tell us what we want to know now or *later*, but you will surely tell'. It's hard for a man not to confess even to what he doesn't know. When they start to squeeze your balls or put electric wires on your . . .

SHARON   Stop, I don't want to know.

SPARROW   I don't want to know either but Van Muellin makes you know. You see there's over twenty million of us and four million of them so that's how they keep us in check. You understand. They make you betray your mother or your brother. You give names of anyone. And you see the joke is that they already have the names but they just torture anyway. Keep the fear spreading.

SHARON   Stay away from him, this guy sounds insane.

SPARROW   He's not insane. We are insane.

SHARON   Why do you say that?

SPARROW   Because he's still alive and we let him live.

SHARON   Come on to bed honey. Later for him. You're not back there anymore. (*Trying to undress him*)

SPARROW   But I am back there. He accuse me of stealing his money. Mucking Boer bastard. I've never been inside his room.

SHARON   Transfer to another ward.

SPARROW   Another ward? I went to England to get away from them and every other white man I meet is South African or Rhodesian. Now I come to the States and what happens. What ward can I transfer to? You don't understand there *is* no other ward.

SHARON   Look, I understand how you feel, baby.

SPARROW   No you don't understand, Bokkie. Nice girl. Drink Coco Cola and go to Disco, go to work and look at television when night comes but you don't understand. It's different there.

SHARON   Look, I grew up in the South, I know what white people can do. It may not be South Africa but it's still South. Everybody walks around with they heads bowed down. Their backs broken from cotton and liquor. My grandfather still can't look a white man in the eye. So what's the difference?

SPARROW   It's different.

SHARON   How's it different? They still lynching niggers. People disappear right here. It's not just South Africa. Yeah I party, I like to have a good time, that don't mean I don't know what's happening. That don't mean I don't check out reality. I'm not telling you not to fight. Fight yes, but don't let them eat you up from inside. You've got to outlive them. Not die with them.

SPARROW   I must deal with this man.

SHARON   You deal with him but not on his terms. On yours. Now come on go to bed. *(She touches him)*

   Darkness

SCENE V

Morning on the ward. Sparrow stands holding a tray of breakfast food which he had collected from a patient.

SPARROW   Morning, Nkosi, and the half eaten bread and porridge of old men who piss themselves.

   (He looks down at tray)

You know, Nkosi, I think America is a hospital and there are many wards.

(Thinks about it)

Yeah many wards and no rewards.

Miss Derris enters

MISS DERRIS   Sparrow, can you come to my office when you get a chance?

Half smile, half nervous tick. Constantly fumbling with pen. She walks over to area of stage which is her office, symbolized by chair and desk.

SPARROW   Well, here it comes, Nkosi. Fired already. Well who wants their bleery job anyhow? Tell them what to do with their hospital, hey don't I say. Let me walk into this white woman's office just like I was sane. Just like all this was real. Just as if there was a beginning a middle and an end to life.

Walks across stage talking to himself until he reaches her desk.

I'll sit down.

Makes the motion of a man about to sit down then notices there is no chair.

No I'll stand.

MISS DERRIS   *(Looking up from papers)* Beg pardon?

SPARROW   You wanted to see me.

MISS DERRIS   Oh yes.

SPARROW   It's about Van Muellin. You want to fire me. I don't mos care.

MISS DERRIS   Oh no, I'm not going to fire you. He's found the money.

SPARROW   He found the money.

MISS DERRIS   Yes, it wasn't stolen after all. What I want to talk to you about is something else.

SPARROW   Something else?

MISS DERRIS   Yes, simply it goes like this. We are here to do a job. The job is to help sick people. When you walk in that hospital door all outside relationships cease. We can't afford the luxury of hatred or prejudice because people die if we do. Do you understand?

SPARROW   Van Muellin . . .

MISS DERRIS   Mr. Van Muellin is a patient and that's all. I don't care if he's South African, Chinese or a Martian, he's a patient and he's here because he's sick.

SPARROW   Yeah he's sick.

MISS DERRIS   You think you have a legitimate right to hate okay. Do you know anything about what the English did to Ireland? They killed, raped and colonized. They used us like toilet paper . . . but still I'm a nurse and my job is the saving of life not the taking of it. Catholic or Protestant, black or white, it has no meaning here.

SPARROW   No meaning.

MISS DERRIS   All that ends at the front door. Do you understand?

SPARROW   I understand.

MISS DERRIS   And by the way if anything were to happen to Mr. Van Muellin we would be very suspicious. Do I make myself clear?

SPARROW   Yes, very clear.

MISS DERRIS   You see as long as he is in this hospital we are responsible for him. Well I won't keep you. I just wanted you to know how things were. Are there any questions?

SPARROW   No.

> (He walks away from desk)

No, no questions, all questions have been answered before they were asked, Nkosi, and all doors shut tight.

Darkness.

SCENE VI
DREAM SEQUENCE

Stage lighting rises on Van Muellin who is seen seated in his wheelchair atop a huge ramp. In his hand he holds his sjambok (a club which the Afrikaners use to club black workers). Next the light rises on Sparrow who is half naked on his knees looking up the ramp to where Van Muellin is seated. Sharon enters from left of stage, slowly wrapping a head tie. Miss Derris enters from right of stage.

SPARROW   What is my crime?

VAN MUELLIN   Treason against the state.

SPARROW   Treason?

VAN MUELLIN   Subversion must be punished Jong.

SHARON   Let him go please, he won't do you any harm. I promise you. He has no gun.

MISS DERRIS   *(Holding rosary beads)* I know a country where the young are broken, where the children beg with running sores, where the pope gave away the land like a parcel and left us religious hungry and poor. Holy Mary Mother of God pray for us sinners now and at the hour of our death.

VAN MUELLIN   It isn't the guns which worry us. We make the guns. He doesn't want to live anymore, that's why he's dangerous. You're not afraid of death are you Jong? We have known about you for some time. You or someone very like you.

SPARROW   What is my crime?

VAN MUELLIN   I told you, treason against the state of South Africa.

SPARROW   Freedom?

VAN MUELLIN   Your freedom is my treason. Now you are a hand, but hands become fists.

SHARON   If you let him go I'll take him away. He'll be no threat to you.

VAN MUELLIN   And what will you do with him girl. Will you lock him up between your thighs? Can you keep his madness away? Can you keep him from being political?

SHARON   I can keep him.

MISS DERRIS   I know a land where the young are broken, where a colonial wind drives each from each. Where only death can bring you honour, but freedom they keep beyond your reach. Say the word and your soul shall be healed. *(Lights three candles)*

VAN MUELLIN   What's the matter with you Jong? You've got a girl there that will keep you in her thighs? And still you want to change things. *(Laughing)*

SPARROW   I want more.

VAN MUELLIN   I'll give you bloody more. You stinking Kaffir bastard. It's the Jews that put these ideas in your head isn't it? The Jews. The Communists. Admit it. We'll send ten thousand volts through your balls and see if you still talk of freedom.

SHARON   *(Screams)* Oh God no please.

MISS DERRIS   Holy Mary mother of God pray for us now and at the hour of our death.

VAN MUELLIN   Who is your mother Kaffir?

SPARROW   Hunger.

VAN MUELLIN   No, the state is your mother, the state gave birth
        to you. When a nigger tries to overthrow the state he is
        trying to kill his mother. Do you understand Blackboy?

SPARROW   No.

SHARON   Tell him you understand.

VAN MUELLIN   Are you a communist, Jong?

SPARROW   America won't help us.

VAN MUELLIN   Are you a communist?

SPARROW   England won't help us.

VAN MUELLIN *(Hysterical)* Are you a communist?

SPARROW   No, I'm a man.

> *Van Muellin raises the sjambok to strike*
>
> *Darkness. Only the 3 candles remain burning*
>
> *Wakes to find Sharon*

SHARON   Sparrow. Sparrow wake up baby, it's all right.

SPARROW   Look look, look they've come. The hippos.

SHARON   Ssh. It's okay. It's okay Sparrow.

SPARROW   Sharon? I was dreaming.

SHARON   You're sweating.

SPARROW   I dreamt

SHARON   What did you dream? You said something about
        Hippos.

SPARROW   Hippos are police cars.

SHARON   You were dreaming about back home again?

SPARROW   Day and night their hands are heavy on me.

SHARON   I have nightmares sometimes too. I dream about my stepfather coming into my room.

SPARROW   Your stepfather.

SHARON   I never liked him. He used to drink a lot. I think he wanted to rape me.

SPARROW   Can't blame him.

She slaps him

Hey!

SHARON   Suppose it was your sister or your daughter. You wouldn't think it was funny. *(Looks at him)* Or if it were you.

SPARROW   I didn't say it was funny, I just say I can't blame him for wanting to.

SHARON   Well I can blame him. If my mother didn't come in I don't know what would have happen. She never said anything about it but we all knew. If he had done it I'd of got him. I don't care how long I had to wait. I'd get him.

SPARROW   Like Van Muellin.

SHARON   That's different.

SPARROW   Why is it different, there's many ways to rape or be raped.

SHARON   That's true I guess. Still it's different for a man.

SPARROW   Come here girl *(He pulls her to him)* I never meant for this to happen you know. Already we know the way the other sleeps. We know the others dreams.

SHARON   And so.

SPARROW   I only wanted to be your lover. When you start to know dreams, then you start to take responsibility.

SHARON   And you don't want responsibility right?

SPARROW   With responsibility comes promises that I can't keep. I don't know how long I'm going to be here. Or even if I'm going to be here. There's something I must do. You see, this America is different.

SHARON   Different?

SPARROW   It's like you smile but you really do not smile. You sleep but you don't really sleep. You can walk where you want to, you don't have to show a pass but still . . .

SHARON   But still what? Say it.

SPARROW   Asleep.

SHARON   Asleep?

SPARROW   *(Looking in her eyes)* Yes, asleep. And you try and pretend that everything is all right but meanwhile . . .

SHARON   A time bomb is going in your brain.

Sparrow and Sharon look out into the audience to see who will betray them. Together they make the sound of the time bomb. With each movement they make the violent contraction which is birth.

SPARROW AND SHARON   Tick . . . Tick . . . Tick . . . Tick . . . Tick . . . Tick . . . Tick . . . Tick . . .

Pause and final

Tick.

They look at each other and disappear in unison beneath blanket.

Darkness.

ACT III

SCENE I

Lights come up on Van Muellin in the hospital in his wheelchair. Miss Derris enters.

VAN MUELLIN   More tests today?

MISS DERRIS   They just want a further urine sample. Here you are, if you please Mr. Van Muellin. Just ring when you're ready. *(Hands him a specimen jar)*

VAN MUELLIN   Test, test, test and still nothing. When will they stop testing and start curing? God what a country.

MISS DERRIS   The doctors are doing the best that they can Mr. Van Muellin.

VAN MUELLIN   Well that's not good enough, I'm still dying.

MISS DERRIS   We're all dying Mr. Van Muellin.

VAN MUELLIN   *(Mimicks her)* 'We're all dying Mr. Van Muellin'. Then why aren't they taking your piss?

She exits angry.

What a bleery country.

He turns wheelchair and urinates into bottle, his back to audience. He turns again and presses button on the wall which summons the nurse. He picks up newspaper – The Times – and begins to read.

Hey, so they threaten sanctions again? Fools. We're ready for them.

He presses button again. Sparrow enters.

SPARROW   Yes.

VAN MUELLIN   Well, Jong, so it's you.

SPARROW   They said you were ringing.

VAN MUELLIN   Yes, my specimen is ready. They say they want it. Here!

Sparrow takes bottle without answering.

I haven't seen much of you Jong. How does it go with you?

SPARROW   It goes.

VAN MUELLIN   I think you hate me Jong.

(No answer)

And yet we are more alike than any here. We understand each other. We come from the same earth. Maybe sucked from the same breast. I had a black nanny in childhood. Tell me why you are here, Jong?

SPARROW   If we're so alike why do you call me Jong?

VAN MUELLIN   I call my son Jong.

SPARROW   I'm not your bloody son.

VAN MUELLIN   Why are your here?

SPARROW   I work, don't I mos.

VAN MUELLIN   Why aren't you home with your people? *(Begins to toy with a sjambok cane which he has)*

SPARROW   You told us we had no home, aint it.

(Looks at sjambok cane)

VAN MUELLIN   We never said you have no home only that your home be separate from us. You come to America for what. You want to marry a white woman?

SPARROW   I have no desire to marry a white woman. Is that all you think of us?

VAN MUELLIN   Then why come here. South Africa is better country, more life, more everything. Here they lie. They feel the same as we do but they lie. They say we have no morality. What does America know about morality. We do the dirty work. We create the money. We dig the diamonds. They don't mind as long as they keep the clean hands and faces. They say a revolution is coming. There will be no revolution in South Africa. You know why?

SPARROW   Why, Menheer? Why do you think there will be no revolution?

VAN MUELLIN   Because we'll do what America did. We'll create a black middle class if necessary. Sure. Maybe one millionaire a year. In twenty years you have twenty. That will be enough to stop all protest. Watch if you think I lie.

SPARROW   You think that will be enough?

VAN MEULLIN   I know it. So now tell me, why are you here?

SPARROW   Because at least I'm not working the mines.

VAN MUELLIN   *(Laughs)* Jong, there are mines and there are mines. *(Pause)* But tell me, how are your papers?

SPARROW   My papers?

VAN MUELLIN   Your papers, are they in order?

SPARROW   You shouldn't worry about my papers, you should worry about your health, *(Pause)* Menheer.

Sparrow exits.

Lights come up slowly on Sharon in the Laboratory. Sparrow walks over to her slowly talking to himself.

SPARROW   There are mines and there are mines. I must kill this man, Nkosi.

SHARON   Say what?

SPARROW   Van Muellin *(Hands her specimen)*

SHARON   Van Muellin again. Just put it down.

SPARROW   I must kill this man right. I must not kill him wrong.
                     He is like a snake you must not touch it but you must kill it.

SHARON   Are you all right?

SPARROW   But my papers aren't in order. They would deport
                     me. I would be tried in South Africa. He knows. But still he
                     must die.

SHARON   Quiet, they'll hear you.

SPARROW   They make black millionaires. Why not? What they
                     make they can crush. You have money but where can you
                     spend the money. What they give you with one hand they
                     take away with the other. Why not give a million in order to
                     make a billion? *(He laughs)*

SHARON   Be cool man, be cool.

SPARROW   Be cool, yeah my sister, cool cool.

*(He suddenly turns and grabs the gold necklace around her
neck. She screams).*

You see this? Gold. For this I was born dead.

SHARON   Listen, Sparrow, quit if it's so painful. Forget the job.

SPARROW   It won't forget me, Sharon. It won't forget me.

(Screaming) Van Muellin!

*Lights come up on Van Muellin and Miss Derris she is
taking his blood pressure in the background while Sparrow
is talking with Sharon in foreground.*

SHARON   Wait listen we'll go to lunch, alright? We have to talk.

SPARROW   I don't want to talk, I must kill this man. You don't
                     understand.

SHARON   Stop saying I don't understand. Look, I don't want any-
                     thing to happen to you. I'm used to you now. Maybe that

sounds selfish but that's what's happening. There have
been a few men in my life I felt this way about, damn few. If
you don't want to stay here you don't have to. If you don't
want to work you don't have to.

SPARROW   This is not staying or going, working or not working.
This is something more. Even when I dream I feel his teeth
in me.

SHARON   Just stay with me, tonight. Stay with me.

He looks at her.

Darkness

SCENE II
LOVE AND THE FIRST HOUR.

*Sparrow in bed with Sharon after making love. She wakes to find
him stirring.*

SHARON   What you thinking?

SPARROW   I was thinking of my sixteen birthday. I was home
then.

SHARON   I remember mine. I wasn't afraid. Nobody could tell me
nothing,boy. I thought I had it all together.

SPARROW   I wanted my birthday alone. They had all my others
for themselves, but my sixteenth was my own. So goodbye
mother, goodbye father. I just ran away by night. I slipped
past the watchman at the corner of the street, and went out
into the bushland. I had no pass to leave the location.

SHARON   You weren't scared.

SPARROW   Oh yes I was scared but it was my birthday, my
sixteenth year. I wanted to be where there was no
whiteman. I slept out beneath the stars. You understand. I

wanted a woman but I wanted the stars more, so I slept
alone.

SHARON   And did you dream?

SPARROW   I dreamt I was an Ogun. As much fire as fire and no
man could hold me.

SHARON   Nice. *(Kisses him)*

SPARROW   My sixteenth year.

SHARON   I must have known you sometime before.

SPARROW   Why?

SHARON   Because if I didn't know you I wouldn't have been able
to just fall asleep beside you. I can never fall asleep with a
strange man. You know, I mean I can . . . but I can't sleep
with somebody new. I'm funny like that. *(Pause)* And what
did you do after that night, your birthday night?

SPARROW   I went back and I cursed them.

SHARON   Who?

SPARROW   All or them. I cursed my mother and asked why she
bore me in the wrong time. The time of our captivity.

SHARON   But she couldn't help it.

SPARROW   You're talking reason. I didn't want reason, I wanted
freedom. Dead, I was free. Unborn I was free, but half born
what was I? I was sixteen and father was forty and still they
called him Jong.

SHARON   Jong?

SPARROW   Boy. You understand. They called him Jong and he
called them Baas. So how could a child make a man. How
could I be a man? But it was my birthday, my sixteenth year
and I couldn't let them have it. Mother don't I mos dead.

She covers him with her body.

SHARON   A letter came for you.

SPARROW   A letter. When did it come?

SHARON   Yesterday, I wasn't going to give it to you.

SPARROW   But why?

SHARON   Because it was from a woman. Don't you understand I
don't want your woman writing here?

SPARROW   Give it to me.

She hands him envelope.

SHARON   *(After a pause).* Well, what does she say?

SPARROW   Here you read it.

Sharon surprized. Takes letter and reads.

SPARROW   Out loud. See what it is you're jealous of.

SHARON   Dear Nephtali,
I hope it is not heavy with you. I got your address from your
mother. She is a good one. The child is well. I got married.
The man was not good. I could not wait on you. I know you
had no wish to marry. I am not with him now. He drinks
and works in the mines when he can. I thought it would do
well for the child but he drinks to forget his work and so he
forgets us too. His people are from Losotho. Your father
has not forgiven me for marrying. He says he would have
taken me and your child into his house. Now that I have
married he says it is different with me. Men are always late
to understand. Things are as you left them here.
The Boers say things will change. They say God loves this
country because he gave us so much. The gold, the
diamonds. But if there were not so much here would they
have let us free long ago.
Why were we so blessed?
Send what you can.

I am with you as you are with me. The child too is of you.
Love Azania Temba.

Sharon looks up from the letter and looks at Sparrow
through the tears in her eyes.

Darkness.

SCENE III

SPARROW   *(Addressing audience)* Yesterday I walked a certain
city, Nkosi. You see, death was in my mouth, in my eyes, so
I walked. I passed so close to things that I thought I was
drunk. What things? Things which call themselves people.
Some were black, some were white. Call them things Nkosi,
it doesn't matter. They too are part of sleep. Some have
mouths like birds. Their heads bent down to the earth.
Their bodies get in your way and interrupt your thoughts.
Your sadness trips over their sadness. I walked their streets,
Nkosi. You too have seen them.
I rode in their buses and trains. Their trains which go under
the earth and into a darkness as deep as the mines of
Johanesburg. I have seen them, Nkosi.
And because I was afraid, I asked:
What city is this and how long must I stay?
And they said, until the end.
And because I was confused I asked:
Until whose end, your end or mine?
The city of Man or the City of God?
But they wouldn't answer, Nkosi.
And their dead eyes said: *accept*
Their broken backs said: *accept*
Their breath stank of liquor: *accept*
Their arms swollen from needles: *accept*
And the young girls with old women's faces accept.
(Pause)

Yesterday I walked a certain city, Nkosi and saw the children of acceptance.

Darkness

The hospital ward. Van Muellin and Nurse Derris.

VAN MUELLIN   You come with another injection for me? My backside feels like a pin cushion.

MISS DERRIS   No more injections just now. I need to take your blood pressure.

VAN MUELLIN   You're not married are you?

MISS DERRIS   No

VAN MUELLIN   I thought not.

MISS DERRIS   What has that to do with your blood pressure? Surely my marital status couldn't concern you one way or the other.

VAN MUELLIN   It has nothing to do with my blood pressure but everything to do with yours.

MISS DERRIS   Maybe I could find another injection for you after all.

VAN MUELLIN   No, no please, I meant no offence.

She begins to strap him for examination.

How long before they can stop all this foolishness and cure me?

MISS DERRIS   It takes time, Mr. Van Muellin, many tests must be done.

VAN MUELLIN   Time. It takes time. What a funny stupid expression.

MISS DERRIS   And why so, Rome wasn't built, in a day surely, nor destroyed in one.

VAN MUELLIN   Time is like a pool of water. It trickles down from the Future which is not real, to the Present which is too quick to be real, into the Past which is no longer real. So none of time is real.

MISS DERRIS   Really?

VAN MUELLIN   But of the three which are unreal, which is the most real?

MISS DERRIS   The present surely.

VAN MUELLIN   No the present is too quick, I can't understand the present. Only the past. Like the early days of South Africa when we were . . . when we had no doubts. And my youth in Germany.

MISS DERRIS   And have you any doubts now?

VAN MUELLIN   I was stupid to come to America. They can't save me. Test and more test. Wonder drugs, radiation therapy and what? This is a foolish country.

MISS DERRIS   There's still a chance.

VAN MUELLIN   A chance. Are you afraid of death, Nurse Derris?

MISS DERRIS   No, not really. I've known it all my life surely. The wakes and the funerals, the wailing we call Keening. I've grown up with it. The white cloth covering mirrors and the widows wearing black. No, death is no stranger to me, or I to it.

Lights go down on them and rises on Sparrow and Sharon.

SHARON   Is there anything I can get her? I'll go shopping tomorrow and mail some clothes. I'll go to Macy's . . .

SPARROW   *(Laughing)* Sharon it's not so simple.

SHARON   Anything she needs I'll send her.

SPARROW   She needs more than a few pairs of panties. She

needs freedom.

SHARON   I can't . . . I can't send that.

SPARROW   No, it can't be given *(Holding her)* You must take that for yourself.

He gets up and begins to dress.

SHARON   Where are you going?

He doesn't answer.

Not yet please, wait until I fall asleep. Lay with me a little while longer. I'm scared.

He lays down with her.

Darkness.

Lights up on hospital

VAN MUELLIN   You should come to South Africa, Miss Derris.

MISS DERRIS   South Africa. Whatever would I do there?

VAN MUELLIN   Just what you do here.

MISS DERRIS   Well, if it's the same thing then why go at all?

VAN MUELLIN   You would love it. It's a beautiful country. God's country. You look at the sunset and you see something. What can you see here.

MISS DERRIS   And what about the black people?

VAN MUELLIN   What about them.

MISS DERRIS   Isn't it their country?

VAN MUELLIN   Don't talk foolishness. We were there first, it's they who are the immigrants.

MISS DERRIS   Well I don't want to discuss it. I have my own land to go to if I ever feel the need to leave America.

VAN MUELLIN   You don't know what you're missing. The Kaffirs are no problem believe me. They're glad for what they can get. Listen, you think New York is a modern city you should see . . .

MISS DERRIS   I think it's time for your enema.

VAN MUELLIN   I don't want any goddamn enema. You just like to torture people.

MISS DERRIS   Its either now or first thing tomorrow morning.

VAN MUELLIN   Tomorrow. Tomorrow, for God's sake.

MISS DERRIS   All right then. Just take these pills like a good boy. And I'll come in later for your injection. There's a good fellow.

VAN MUELLIN   (Swallowing pills) Blinken Christ.

Lights on Sparrow – he sees that Sharon is sleeping. The sound of South African voices are heard. They build to a crescendo and plague him until he must run out.

SPARROW   If not now, when, Nkosi? If not me then who?

Darkness.

SCENE IV

The Hospital. Sparrow enters Van Muellin's room. The voices continue in Sparrow's brain. Van Muellin is in his wheelchair reading. The Sjambok cane is beside him on the floor.

VAN MUELLIN   Well Peter Claus, I see you can't sleep either.

SPARROW   It's you who stop my sleep, Van Muellin.

VAN MUELLIN   How can I stop your sleep, Jong?

SPARROW   You should be dead. A thing like you.

VAN MUELLIN   *(Grabbing sjambok)* Stay away from me Kaffir. I
knew from the first what you had in mind. Come, you will
see that it won't be that easy. Come, Jong!

*Sparrow pulls Van Muellin up from wheelchair as Van
Muellin swings at him with the Sjambok. As Van Muellin
stands we see the plastic bag which contains his urine. It
hangs from him as the hospital robe reveals his almost
naked body. Sparrow begins to strangle Van Muellin from
behind, taking the sjambok up about his throat. Van
Muellin screams.*

VAN MUELLIN   Help! Help me! The Kaffir . . .

SPARROW   You find us funny, Menheer. Laugh Baas. Laugh at
Peter Claus.

Miss Derris enters.

MISS DERRIS   What are you doing? My God. Let him go! Let him
go!

SPARROW   Let him go? Yes I'll let him go.

MISS DERRIS   He's dying.

SPARROW   Yes.

MISS DERRIS   He has cancer. There is no need to kill him. He's
dying anyway.Do you hear what I'm saying. He is dying
anyway.

SPARROW   *(Suddenly releasing him)* Are you sure?

MISS DERRIS   Yes, I'm certain. There is no chance for him.

SPARROW   Will it be a slow death?

MISS DERRIS   Yes.

SPARROW   And painful.

MISS DERRIS   Very painful.

SPARROW   All right then. *(He lets him drop into his wheelchair)*

MISS DERRIS   He is no longer a threat. He's not worth your life.

Sparrow exits.

VAN MUELLIN   *(Drinking water which she gives him)* You should have let him kill me.

MISS DERRIS   Let him kill you?

VAN MUELLIN   They would have written about me in *The Rand Daily*. Now who will write about an old man dead of cancer? They'll give me five lines. Five lines after I gave so much. The Ossewa Brandwag. The Society of Honour. You did wrong to expose my illness before him. We must never appear weak. Once they see us shaken we are lost.

MISS DERRIS   Do you want me to call him back?

VAN MUELLIN   You wouldn't understand. What do you know of honour? You Irish know only how to empty chamber pots and sing.

MISS DERRIS   *(Slaps him)* You eegit. Can't you understand its over? Done. The way you live. It's over. You can't go dreaming forever. The world's not like that anymore, you can't rule people's lives anymore as if they were cattle or pieces of shit that God threw away. Because they'll bloody kill you one night. Maybe not this night, maybe not that night but one night surely. I mean England tried it, the French tried it, the Belgians tried it . . .

VAN MUELLIN   We are not trying it Miss Derris, we are *doing* it.

MISS DERRIS   *(Turns to go and looks back at him)* One night, maybe not this night or that night but one night surely.

Light darkens as she exits and rises on Sparrow.

SPARROW   New York New York, city of gold don't I say. Jo'Burg, New York, London, Amsterdam, Zurich, Paris, Moscow. Seven cities of gold. Shall I fear you? Shall I fear you? You have hands and faces, your currency and power.

Shall I fear you?
The Lord is my light and my salvation, Nkosi.
Whom shall I fear.
When they came to eat my flesh
They stumbled and fell.
My soul escaped as a bird out of the snare of the fowler.
The snare is broken and my very soul escaped.
If you can't slay the old men then you must slay the
children.
You hide but they will not let you hide Nkosi.

He laughs

They kill you if you work
They kill you if you do not work
But always they kill you.
I wanted to paint pictures, Nkosi, but they don't understand
painting. Only gold.
So now I must paint what they can understand.

He puts gold paint on his face

There are mines and there are mines.
The weather in the white man's soul.
You know Nkosi, there is only one reason why they call us
boys.

He laughs.

When you call a man a boy you only have to pay him a
boy's wages. How clever they are Nkosi, clever eh, my God,
don't I say.

*Laughs and lets build until the audience joins him in the
infectious mirth and then suddenly he brings on a stillness.*

If my father has the petrol,
Then my mother has the match.
If my father was the cruxifixion,
Then I must be the resurrection.

TSHOSHALOZA

Slow darkness.

Music: Tshoshaloza is heard.

CURTAIN

TRINITY –

The Long and Cheerful Road to Slavery

for C L R James

These three one-act plays were first performed at the Riverside
Studio, London, February 25 to March 14, 1982.

MAN AND SOUL

Faigan .... Victor Romero Evans
Ikuru .... Burt Caesar
Policeman .... Melvyn Jones

THE CASE OF DR KOLA

Dr Kola .... Gordon Case
Sgt Kay .... Victor Romero Evans

THAT GENERATION

Wallace .... Gordon Case
Phyllis .... Decima Francis
Carol .... Beverley Martin

Directed by Charlie Hanson
Assistant to Director Bella Freud

MAN AND SOUL

CAST

Faigan .... A West-Indian
Thomas Ikuru .... An African student
Policeman .... White

The play opens in a detention cell in London. The time is late
August during the Notting Hill Carnival.

SCENE I

POLICEMAN   In there, mate. *(Pushing Faigan)*

FAIGAN   Look, you don't have to push me, right?

POLICEMAN   You too *(To Thomas)*.

THOMAS   I am telling you that you have made a mistake. I don't
belong here. I am not even one of them.

POLICEMAN   Sure, sure. Pull the other one, it's got bells on it.

THOMAS   I am an African. I'm not West-Indian. Call my con-
sulate.

POLICEMAN   Tomorrow you can call your bloody witch doctor
for all I care, but for now *(Shoving Thomas)* you sleep in
there. *(Exit policeman)*

FAIGAN   *(Laughing)* So you not one of us, eh? You catch a lash
in you ass same way.

THOMAS   It is not fair. *(Calling to police)* Look at the way I am
dressed and look at him. *(Faigan is dressed in red trousers
and shirt, Thomas is dressed in suit and tie)* I tell you I only
came to the Carnival to observe.

FAIGAN   Well, you not observing no more, brother, you is it. You
may as well rest you'self.

THOMAS   *(Sits down in despair)* I should not have gone to the
Carnival. My friends warned me. They said you West-
Indians always cause trouble.

FAIGAN   Is what bloodclaat trouble we cause? You see me cause
trouble?

THOMAS   They told me you people draw trouble like a magnet. Is
better to watch you on television.

FAIGAN   But hear this rass fool no.

THOMAS   I am innocent. I was only standing in the crowd

watching when suddenly this fight started. I never threw any
bottle at any police *(Says this loudly)*.

FAIGAN   Is who you telling, God?

THOMAS   I am a student.

FAIGAN   I'm a welder, so what? You rass still lock up here with
me same way. Why don't you stop you crying and let man
hold some peace no.

THOMAS   *(After a pause gets up and looks about him
suspiciously)* Do you think they will beat us? I have heard
that they beat you at night.

FAIGAN   Well, if they try and beat me, they going have for kill me,
tell you that.

THOMAS   This is a bad business. I should have watered my Ike
tree this morning.

FAIGAN   Your what tree?

THOMAS   My Ike tree. You wouldn't understand. Your people
don't deal with our rituals.

FAIGAN   Your people, your people, your people. I tired hearing
that now. To this English man there is only two type of
people – white people and wogs. And you sure as hell not
white.

THOMAS   Well, at least I'm not West-Indian.

FAIGAN   Look, the two of we go clash here tonight if you don't
watch good. I tell you to rest that shit. I don't want to hear
that no more.

THOMAS   All right, all right, I don't mean to insult your people. I
am sorry.

FAIGAN   To hear you Africans you'd think is we who jump up
and say we want to be slaves. Is you who betray we, your
own brothers. Is you who send we here to this shit hole of a

Babylon which they does call Europe. And now you want to turn around and spit upon us because we's not African. You fuckers. You see how war does start.

THOMAS   I am sorry. Please, please don' go on so. You are too sensitive. I did not mean –

FAIGAN   You did not mean. A West-Indian is just a dog to you. A slave and a son of a slave, but you don't mind jumping in bed with one of we women though. They good enough for that, ain't it?

THOMAS   *(Tries to hush Faigan)* Ssh . . . I only meant that we have different ways to see the world.

FAIGAN   Different how? You does eat mealie mealie and Fu Fu, Tapioca and Garri. I does eat rice and peas and saltfish. So how we different?

THOMAS   You know our food.

FAIGAN   Sure, we does buy from the same market in Brixton, ain't it?

THOMAS   Well, when I say different, I am a Muslim.

FAIGAN   So what. I'm a black Jew.

THOMAS   Are you really a Jew?

FAIGAN   Cho! Religion is the last thing me going worry about. You think God even know any of we here? *(He reaches inside of his crutch and takes out a small folded package).*

THOMAS   *(Kneels to pray and looks over his shoulder at Faigan)* What's that?

FAIGAN   Ganja, what you think it is?

THOMAS   That's dangerous, you know. If they catch you –

FAIGAN   They're not going to catch me.

THOMAS   You're not going to smoke that here, are you?

FAIGAN   Shut you fat-hole no man.

THOMAS   What are you doing, eating it?

FAIGAN   What it look like, you don't think I'm going throw it away, do you?

THOMAS   What does that do?

FAIGAN   Ganja come from Africa, man. Is you should know.

THOMAS   I've always stayed far from all that. My father tell me it could drive you mad.

FAIGAN   Being poor could drive you mad. Did you father tell you that?

THOMAS   No.

FAIGAN   Well, then, he didn't tell you what he should have tell you.

THOMAS   *(Childlike)* What does it do?

FAIGAN   What does it do? *(He starts to take off shoes and stretch out on the bench)* It make you feel that you free even though you know that you not free a bloodclaat really. It make you feel as if God ain't forget you even though you know He never even self hear that you was ever born. That's what it does do.

Darkness

SCENE II
DIALOGUE BETWEEN SELF AND SOLE

Faigan looks at the hole in his worn shoes and laughs. Thomas is asleep.

FAIGAN   Between and between is the way we live between and between of things.

The gate of worry and the wailing wall.
(Looking at shoes)
It's a long way we come shoes
is a hard way we come sole.
The debt was there before we born
The debt was there
So is I must pay it.

And father never said
and mother never know
Just how the runnings go.

Between and between
that's the way we live
and yet try hard not to show it.

SCENE III

Later that night

THOMAS   *(Coming over to cot upon which Faigan is sleeping)*
   Are you asleep?

FAIGAN   Not no more I'm not.

THOMAS   I am sorry, I've disturbed you.

FAIGAN   So what happens now?

THOMAS   I can't sleep. I think we should talk.

FAIGAN   What you want to talk about?

THOMAS   Well, we might die here and I don't even know your
   name.

FAIGAN   So if you know my name, you go dead easier?

THOMAS   Well –

FAIGAN   My name is Faigan.

THOMAS.   Faigan, is that your first name or your last?

FAIGAN   Don't worry with all that first and last business, is just
          Faigan. What's yours?

THOMAS   Thomas, Thomas Ikuru.

FAIGAN   Ik who roo?

THOMAS   No, no, Ikuru.

FAIGAN   So is what you doing here, Ik who roo?

THOMAS   Well, I'm in prison, I think.

FAIGAN   I mean what are you doing in England?

THOMAS   Well, I come to study English. My father said that I –

FAIGAN   Should come and learn the white man's magic.

THOMAS   He said it was important that I learn English.

FAIGAN   England is a funny place, boy. People come either to
          study or to hide.

THOMAS   Well, I come to study.

FAIGAN   First you study and then you hide.

THOMAS   I don't understand.

FAIGAN   You will. So how your studying going so far?

THOMAS   Well, I want to take a degree in economics first and
          then in law.

FAIGAN   You should have take the law first and then the
          economics.

THOMAS   You think so?

FAIGAN   Sure. If you would have take the law first you rass might
          not have land here.

THOMAS   Do you think they will do anything to us?

FAIGAN   They would try. But tell me something, Ik who roo.

THOMAS   Ikuru, Thomas Ikuru.

FAIGAN   Is how long you plan on keeping on that jacket and tie?
    You not hot?

THOMAS   No.

FAIGAN   You could sleep with that thing round you neck?

THOMAS   Yes.

FAIGAN   Well, sleep then, I tired. *(Curls back up again on cot)*

THOMAS   Do you think they would let me write a letter?

FAIGAN   Sure you could write.

THOMAS   I want to let my wife know in case something . . .
    happens to me.

FAIGAN   Listen, it's no big thing, they haven't charged us yet. This
    is just a detention cell. If it was anything heavy they would
    have take away you tie and belt first thing.

THOMAS   Why?

FAIGAN   So they don't have to worry about you hanging you self.

THOMAS   *(Frightened)* Hang myself?

FAIGAN   Listen, just relax, get some sleep, tomorrow you reach
    your wife and she come see about getting you out.

THOMAS   But she is not here.

FAIGAN   So where is she?

THOMAS   Nigeria.

FAIGAN   Bloodclaat.

THOMAS   I haven't seen her in two years.

FAIGAN   Two years? You sure she still your wife?

THOMAS   Oh yes, she is very . . . F-A-I-T-H-F-U-L.

FAIGAN   She more than that if she stay true to you for all this
time.

THOMAS   I too have been faithful, no woman for two years.

FAIGAN   What? Boy, you good. I can't go two weeks without a
rub, never mind two years. Is what you do, yoga?

THOMAS   I would never touch one of these English girls, you
don't know who they've been with. You can't even tell what
they put in their mouths. You could catch something.

FAIGAN   Two years. So what, you just a study, study, study and
thing?

THOMAS   Yes.

FAIGAN   So what you does do when pressure reach you?

THOMAS   Pressure?

FAIGAN   Yes, man, pressure in you ass. When the white man say
no.

THOMAS   No.

FAIGAN   Right, No! No money, no help, no life, no joy, no
nothing but pure licks in the ass.

THOMAS   Licks? *(Faigan makes the pantomime motion of
someone being whipped)* Oh, you mean lash.

FAIGAN   Lash, licks, whipping, whatever you want call it. Is the
same thing, pressure. Except here the white man does do it
different.

THOMAS   How you mean?

FAIGAN   Well, he won't beat you regular the same way because
you see after a while you does get use to it so you know
when to tighten up your bati?

THOMAS   Tighten your bati?

FAIGAN   Yes, you make yourself ready because you know it
coming. So what they do now is change the rhythm so that
you *never* know just how the stroke going to land. Just
when you think it coming he let you go. Like maybe he let
you marry one of his woman, or maybe he let you be the
only black man on a job, and because he let you hold a
work you feel say he might really like you, or maybe they
are not all the same. Maybe he changes from Labour to
Tory or Tory to Labour, and then it comes –

THOMAS   The lash?

FAIGAN   In you ass. If it's a job they make sure you have no
power. If it's a woman, then she's just there to keep you in
check.

THOMAS   But how can a woman keep a man in check?

FAIGAN   You will learn, brother, you will learn. *(Goes down on
the floor to do sit up exercises).*

THOMAS   So, what are you doing here in England?

FAIGAN   I'm a welder, ain't I? You a student, I'm a welder.

THOMAS   No, I don't mean what job do you do, I mean *why* are
you here?

FAIGAN   Well, me mother bring me from small.

THOMAS   Well, you could go.

FAIGAN   Not so easy you know, brother.

THOMAS   I don't believe you really want to go. If I really wanted to
leave some place I would leave.

FAIGAN   *(Suddenly stops exercising)* You see that pussclaat door
there?

THOMAS   Yes, I see it.

FAIGAN   Is why you don't open it?

THOMAS   Because I don't have a key.

FAIGAN   Well, is the same reason I can't left England. Money is
         the key, money is the door, money is the pressure in you
         ass, you understand now?

THOMAS   Yes, I understand.

FAIGAN   Good, I glad.

THOMAS   *(Pauses)* You know . . . there once was a man who
         went outside of his hut at night to make water.

FAIGAN   To make water, and what happen?

THOMAS   He was never seen again.

FAIGAN   *(Laughing)* Ik who roo, you is a jester.

THOMAS   Ikuru. I-K-U-R-U. *(Takes off jacket and tie and lays
         down to sleep)*

FAIGAN   Yeah, right.

THOMAS   Faigan?

FAIGAN   What now?

THOMAS   I just want you to know . . . it was not I who sold you
         into slavery. Please don't hold me responsible.

FAIGAN   Well, someone sure as hell did.

         Darkness

SCENE IV
FATHER YOU SAY THAT WE COME FROM SLEEP

THOMAS   What am I doing here father,
         you who sent me here.
         You say we all come from sleep

am I to be the dreamer or the dream.

You say it's not enough that we be
hewers of wood
drawers of water.
We must take our place
no longer the kept but also the keepers of our fate
and destiny is a word
which must come to rest in our mouths.

You say we all come from sleep
am I to be the dreamer or the dream.

Darkness

SCENE V
THE LAYING ON OF HANDS

THOMAS   You know what we must do, Faigan?

FAIGAN   No, star, you tell me.

THOMAS   We must learn to become more like the Englishman.
            You see that when he come to Africa, he just comes to take
            what he needs. Gold, diamonds, silver, even people.
            It's all a matter of import and export to him, whether its
            cocoa or human beings. He knows that in Africa any white
            man can come wearing khaki and leave wearing silk. If he
            has no conscience, I mean.

FAIGAN   He's a beast, how can he have a conscience?

THOMAS   Well, we must learn to become the same way. When we
            come here to England, we should not concern ourselves
            with anything but making what we can and getting the hell
            out. We should not bother with the politics or Parliament or
            these law courts because we can never win. Leave them to
            it. Let them die. Import and export.

FAIGAN   Well, I don't mind leave, you know. It's just that . . .

THOMAS   What?

FAIGAN   Just as long as it's me that make the choice. I don't want
to feel that it's them drive me away. Because it's then that I
say me no leave the area, to Royal George.

THOMAS   You see what I mean? You still want to fight them.
Forget them. Take what you need and run, the way they
do.

FAIGAN   They don't run. They walk. What do they call it? An
orderly retreat. But tell me something, Ikuru. Why is that
when a country gets rich, the people still stay poor?

THOMAS   Well, the more money in circulation, the higher things
become.

FAIGAN   But what about the people in the Bush, the people who
live back-a-yard?

THOMAS   Well, they move from the village to the city and because
they want to buy nice things, they work a little harder.

FAIGAN   But no matter how hard they work, things are always
coming more expensive. It's like a man chasing his own
shadow. You can never catch it.

Lighting makes shadow on wall.

THOMAS   Look, Faigan. We have the same hand.

FAIGAN   What?

THOMAS   Look there, the same size. We might have been from
the same tribe or the same family, if things had not happen,
I mean. *(Touching Faigan's hand to his).*

FAIGAN   *(Angry)* If I don't deal with if. If shit had wings, then a
dog would fly. You ever hear that? *I* not *if* hungry. I *am*
hungry.

THOMAS   Look, Faigan. You must be patient with me. I am at
least trying. It is not easy for me. I was raised another kind

of way. My father was very strict with me. He had to meet all of my friends to decide on them. If he ever found me with my hands in my pockets, he would have the pockets sewn up to teach me a lesson. He was very strict.

FAIGAN   So, in other words you would have never met people like me.

THOMAS   No. Never. But let me say this. Today, when I was at the Carnival and when I saw the police, what they did, I . . . just found myself throwing something, I don't even know what. *(Holding Faigan)* You see I am with you, Faigan. With you. But it frightens me.

FAIGAN   Yes, but when you see me, you see your shame.

   Darkness

SCENE VI
MAN AND GOD

Faigan and Thomas are down on their knees scrubbing the floor of their cell. The time is morning.

THOMAS   I don't see why we must do this.

FAIGAN   Be glad for the exercise.

THOMAS   But I don't see why –

FAIGAN   Is the first time you scrub a floor?

THOMAS   No, I've scrubbed floors before, but that was in my father's house among my own people.

FAIGAN   Well, you not in your father's house now, star. *(Sings)* And is pressure, pressure in you ass.

THOMAS   To rass.

FAIGAN   Is pressure, pressure in you ass.

THOMAS   To rass.

FAIGAN   Good, you learning quick, boy. You know what I been meaning to ask you Ik who roo?

THOMAS   Ikuru. I-K-U-R-U.

FAIGAN   Right. I does see a lot of you fellows driving around in Mercedes car with chauffeur and thing.

THOMAS   And?

FAIGAN   Well, life seem to be going well sweet. Rolls Royce and Mercedes, big cigar stuck in they mouth. Now I hear that back home the people them a eat dust and dog.

THOMAS   Dust and dog?

FAIGAN   Right, most folks catching hell.

THOMAS   Like everywhere in the world the poor are always with us.

FAIGAN   The poor are always with us. That's good, I like that, but how you think they feel to know that one of them big boy cars cost more than they could ever make in they whole lifetime of work?

THOMAS   I don't know.

FAIGAN   Well, you better start for know, you a study economics, ain't it.

THOMAS   I don't run the government.

FAIGAN   But when you a reach home and you is a star boy with degrees and thing in you suitcase, they may well put you in charge.

THOMAS   Well, I'll serve to the best of my ability.

FAIGAN   I hope so. I hope you remember this cell and this floor. Still, you not so bad, at least you not taking home some English woman on you arm.

THOMAS   Africa will take care of Africa's problem. Only an African can understand.

FAIGAN   Well, don't sell the West-Indies cheap. We may play the fool but don't forget Garvey and Padmore. All of them right there with you. *(Thomas looks at him)* It's a funny world, you know.

THOMAS   The world is funny, yes.

FAIGAN   Tell me how you feel about music?

THOMAS   Music, oh yes, I like music.

FAIGAN   No man, the white man does like music. Do you *love* music?

THOMAS   Well, yes, I love music.

FAIGAN   Sometimes I does feel so sad I want dead, you know what I mean? Sometimes the only reason I bother to live is for music. I love me rhythm hard and me melody sweet. I could listen to anything as long as it move me, but it have to be real. Soon as they play a false note I know say it's bullshit.

THOMAS   I grew up with nothing but music around me. In the morning, while I worked, while I played, even when I slept. The world was different then. I miss it.

FAIGAN   So many games in this world they make you play. They never ask you.

THOMAS   Games?

FAIGAN   Sure man. There's games you play by yourself. One person games. That's the game of starvation. You can play that anywhere. In a room, in a street, in a field, anywhere. You just stand still and watch yourself starve. When you get so thin that the watch on your hand drops off you sell it. If you don't have no watch you sell your clothes, your shoes, any damn thing.

THOMAS   Sometime you must sell even the prayer blanket.

FAIGAN   You sell any damn thing, but you stay alive.

THOMAS   But you try and keep your honour.

FAIGAN   Honour? That's something that them fellows like
Mountbatten can deal with. People who could race yacht
and play polo and things in the midst of war. I don't know
nothing about that. Honour is for when you done eat and
there's still something left on the plate. That's when you
can make speech and see whether you tie match your shirt.
Then you could deal with honour.

THOMAS   And what's the game of two people?

FAIGAN   Well, that's love, of course.

THOMAS   And you believe in love?

FAIGAN   Sure, if I can believe in God then I could believe in any
damn thing. Yes, I believe in love. Why not? I ain't no beast.
Love is something you can think about when you done eat.

THOMAS   *(Laughing)* Like honour.

FAIGAN   Well, if you want me to lie to you, I'll lie.

THOMAS   No, I don't want you to lie.

FAIGAN   Well then . . . It's funny to me that the white man come
to teach we words like God and Love. Things like that he
don't have a clue as to what they mean. Think about it.
How could a beast who knows nothing but power, con-
quest and greed come to conceive of something like God?
The word sound funny in his mouth don't it? The only thing
he knows is 'this is beautiful, I must own it'. Is we who teach
him God, and then he comes and teaches it back to us
again, only this time is a different God. A God who says
you must be happy to stay where you are so you can keep
him where he is. You can laugh, you can sing, you can only
have one woman and above all, you must work – hard.

THOMAS   For him?

FAIGAN   Always for him. So they mad, so they sad and they
call himself civilized. And so they drive you to the
ultimate game.

THOMAS   The ultimate game?

FAIGAN   Pimping.

THOMAS   What is pimping?

FAIGAN   Well, brother Rat. You see, when they bring we out of
Africa, I mean we who come by sea and slavery, we come
with nothing but chains and language and even that they
stamped out, to rass.

Who had mother soon lose mother,
who had sister soon lose sister
because they mash-up the family.

They make it so that you have no way to talk and still we
not talking. They only way to communicate is in bed with
you woman and even she can't understand. You see, is not
the woman the white man want to destroy, is the man. Was
always so. Is the man-ness of you which he fear. All he want
do with she is breed her, but you now . . . *(Faigan stands
up, leaving Thomas still on his knees)* You he must destroy
completely. So now when we come to learn this, that's
when we start to use the game. We learned how to live off
our women.

THOMAS   *(Stands up)* It is not right that a man should live off a
woman.

FAIGAN   I not talking what's right, I talking what's real. If you can
find a next way to do it you good. I can't. I not saying that I
won't work if I could. I search for work, but when times
come hard and I have for scuffle and scrunt, well then is to
the woman I looking to help me.

THOMAS   I don't know, if I had to depend upon a woman . . . it

would shame me. I think I would rather to die. Yes, better
to die.

FAIGAN   Well, if you want dead is no problem. From the time we
reach this place they want for kill me. From time, they want
we dead. But I not going dead. Call me what you want, but
I going survive. You don't really know the beast yet.

THOMAS   My father said that man is all. When death comes you
can call for gold and it will not come. You call for silver it
will not come. Only man answers and so a man must be a
man.

FAIGAN   Your father talk good, but you father not here.

THOMAS   You have children?

FAIGAN   I have pickney them yes. Seem like every woman you
meet here got some baby somewhere. Either she pushing
pram or she mother take it and keeping them back home
in the Islands. Is hard for a man not to be father. When she
tell you baby yours all you can say is good, what more you
could say?

THOMAS   And do you want your children to grow up to live off
women?

FAIGAN   I want them to live.

THOMAS   You must know where you come from in order to
know where you are going.

FAIGAN   I know where I came from and I know I can't go back
there without money. Can you tell me any different?
(Thomas doesn't answer him) Right, pressure in you arse.
(Goes back to scrubbing floor)

THOMAS   *(Joining him)* To Rass.

*They laugh together. After a pause, the lighting changes
as the mood changes.*

FAIGAN   *(Becoming quite serious.)* You know what happened

first, the desert moved on us, and then the white man
moved on us and he laughed when we laughed but when we
stopped laughing and asked for freedom he stopped laughing
too, and spoke with guns. And so we spent four hundred
years in shock and it took four hundred years for you to
see me.

THOMAS   I see you, my brother.

Policeman enters

POLICEMAN   Okay, you lot can go now. There's no charges.

THOMAS   Just so? Is that it then?

FAIGAN   About time, I think we should get a public apology, like
St Paul.

POLICEMAN   Not bloody likely, mate. Hurry up. You can pick up
your gear at the desk. *(He exists)*

THOMAS   Well, we're free. *(Starts to laugh)*

FAIGAN   For now.

THOMAS   Look, we'll have to get together again, eh? Keep in
touch. Here, let me write my address on this card. *(Writes
on card and gives it to Faigan)*

FAIGAN   All right, Ik who roo. Hampstead.

THOMAS   Ikuru, I-K-U-R-U.

FAIGAN   Walk good.

THOMAS   We'll get together, have some drinks. *(Fixes tie, and
then shakes Faigan's hand)* Stay in touch, eh? Look at me,
I need a shave. I feel like a bushman. Well, see you, eh?
(He exits)

FAIGAN   *(Alone now, looks around him at cell and begins to
gather up his things)*
On one side of us the desert
on the other the white man

and in between us four hundred years of shock
four hundred years it took us to see
each other.
(Looks at card and laughs)
Hampstead!
(He exits slowly)

Darkness

THE CASE OF DR KOLA

CAST
Sergeant Kay .... Military leader after coup
Dr Kola .... Head of Health Ministry in an African state

Setting: A cell somewhere in Africa.

DR KOLA   *(Reading Bible)* Out of the depths have I cried unto
thee. O Lord.
Lord hear my voice: Let thine ears be
attentive to the voice of my supplications.

*Sergeant enters wearing fatigues and dark shades, carrying
dossier*

SGT KAY   Well, Doctor, reading our Bible, I see.

DR KOLA   At last. Maybe you can sort this business out. There's
been some mistake.

SGT KAY   Mistake?

DR KOLA   Yes, if you could just contact the Chief Minister.

SGT KAY   I'm afraid that would be impossible.

DR KOLA   Well, he could straighten this whole business out.

SGT KAY   You're sure of that, are you?

DR KOLA   They told me that they only wanted to ask me for some
information. They said it wouldn't take more than an hour.
It's been two days since they brought me here. No one has
said anything to me. Why am I being detained?

SGT KAY   Have you been fed?

DR KOLA   Well, they brought me something I guess you could call
food.

SGT KAY   You're very lucky – some of our people are eating
dogs.

DR KOLA   *(Excited)* I demand to know why I'm being detained. I
demand that you put me in touch with the Chief Minister.

SGT KAY   *(Calmly)* Sit down, please.

DR KOLA   I demand to know –

SGT KAY   You'll demand nothing. Sit your arse down. NOW!

DR KOLA   *(Sits down)* Please, the Chief Minister –

SGT KAY   Is no longer with us.

DR KOLA   No longer with us?

SGT KAY   He has been deposed.

DR KOLA   Deposed?

SGT KAY   Unfortunately he attempted to resist arrest and was
           shot.

DR KOLA   Killed . . . But he was just an old man, he couldn't –

SGT KAY   No sir, he was more than just an old man, he was an
           oppressor. I would have preferred that he was not killed,
           but he was very foolish. In any event, do not weep for him.
           You would do better to worry about your own defence.

DR KOLA   My defence?

SGT KAY   There has been a coup and all former members of
           government must stand trial.

DR KOLA   But who is in charge?

SGT KAY   I am.

DR KOLA   You . . . But you're so . . .

SGT KAY   So young, so black?

DR KOLA   I wasn't going to say that, but why . . . no . . . no when
           am I to be tried, who are my accusers? *(Sound of gunfire)*

SGT KAY   You are being tried now, by me.

DR KOLA   And who exactly are you?

SGT KAY   Not that it matters to you, but I am Sergeant Kay. We've
           met before, but you could hardly remember.

DR KOLA   We've met before?

SGT KAY   Not formally. *(Begins to look through papers)*

DR KOLA   I don't understand.

SGT KAY   You will. You are Dr Milton Kola, born in the village of
Sako, educated Royal College and Oxford University,
England. You also studied at Trinity College, Dublin,
Ireland, is that correct?

DR KOLA   Yes. May I smoke?

SGT KAY   Of course.

DR KOLA   No . . . I shouldn't, never mind, I've been trying to stop.
(Pause) My health. *(Sound of gunfire)*

SGT KAY   Your health should be the least of your worries, Doctor.
(Dr Kola tries to light a cigar. The soldier lights it for him)

DR KOLA   Thank you.

SGT KAY   You are 56 years old. Is that correct?

DR KOLA   Yes.

SGT KAY   A wife and three children, all living abroad.

DR KOLA   My wife prefers England, she has a delicate condition
which –

SGT KAY   Your eldest daughter is in boarding school in Lucerne.

DR KOLA   Yes, she's a very good student, majoring in languages.

SGT KAY   I'm sure she knows all of them except her own.

DR KOLA   Well, she's never really spent much time here, you see,
she –

SGT KAY   All of your family are living quite comfortably, wouldn't
you say, Dr Kola?

DR KOLA   Well, I . . . Yes, I guess you could say that they live . . .
comfortably.

SGT KAY   Two cars, a home in Knightsbridge, London, another
in Lucerne. You have a son living in America?

DR KOLA   Yes, he attends school there – Harvard.

SGT KAY   Of course. Your entire family in fact live very pleasant, tax exempt lives.

DR KOLA   No more so than any other cabinet minister! I don't see why I should be accused. I at least live and work here.

SGT KAY   Yes, I know there are those who are never here; you only take three trips a year to Europe.

DR KOLA   To see my family.

SGT KAY   Yes, I know, your wife's delicate condition. Tell me, Doctor, has any member of your family every worked a day in their lives?

DR KOLA   Work?

SGT KAY   Yes, Doctor, work as in labour. You know, use their hands. *(Seizing him.)*

DR KOLA   Well, I don't know . . . My wife came from a rather well-to-do family. She certainly was not raised to –

SGT KAY   Work, don't be afraid of the word. Yes, we know about your wife's family. They were rather better than your own, weren't they?

DR KOLA   I don't think that's any of your business.

SGT KAY   Everything in your life is my business. My interest in your life is all that's keeping you alive.

DR KOLA   All right, all right, forgive me. I'll tell you then. She has constantly flung it in my face that her family was above mine. Because we came from a village and she from the town, she feels superios. One generation before that they were farmers and peasants, yet she feels that she has always done me a favour by marrying me. And the only reason, the only reason she married me was to get into a better class. I was the one who was a doctor; her parents were merely merchants. If truth be told, I did her a service, not vice versa. *(He begins to pace)*

SGT KAY   Calm down, Doctor. We already know your marriage was not made in heaven.

DR KOLA   Not made in heaven? That bitch has made my life one – well, no matter. Tell me, do you know if she has a lover in London? . . . Naturally everyone has a lover in London. I really don't want to know.

SGT KAY   Then why do you ask?

DR KOLA   When I took her there the only English she knew was 'Harrods' and 'credit card'. She soon learned though.

SGT KAY   Well, your little bourgeois problems are not what concern me.

DR KOLA   No, of course not. You don't kill a man because of his wife, do you?

SGT KAY   Tell me, Mr Kola, do you consider yourself a good doctor?

DR KOLA   *(Surprised)* A good doctor? Well, yes, I think I'm competent. I certainly didn't buy my degrees like some people I can name.

SGT KAY   I'm sure you can.

DR KOLA   I haven't really practised medicine for over fifteen years now. I function mainly as an adviser.

SGT KAY   Yes, of course, as an adviser. Tell me, Doctor, you don't remember a certain woman who came to you to see you one night? She had a child with her. She asked you to treat her husband because he seemed to be dying. The woman came from the village of Sako, the same as you.

DR KOLA   ˙I can't be expected to remember every woman who came to me for treatment.

SGT KAY   Naturally, it was some time ago.

DR KOLA   You say the woman came from the village?

SGT KAY   Yes, she told you that she had once served your
mother.

DR KOLA   So many say that, they say anything when they want
help.

SGT KAY   Of course, of course *(Pause)* Well, that woman was my
mother. I was the boy and it was my father who died when
you sent us away. *(Dr Kola lights a cigarette now, his cigar
having gone out)*

DR KOLA   Listen, do you have any idea how many . . . how many
people come to me now? I am not a physician, I am an
official. I can't be expected to –

SGTKAY   You told her to go and see a village doctor, but there
was not village doctor. You knew that.

DR KOLA   There is a doctor there now.

SGT KAY   Now, yes, there is someone who gives out aspirin and
chases all the girls in the village when he's not too drunk to
stand. Dr Linton. But at that time there was no one at all.

DR KOLA   Dr Linton, you say? *(Takes out notebook and gold
fountain pen)* I'll see to it that he is removed.

SGT KAY   I've already seen to it.

DR KOLA   Oh . . . *(Closes notebook and puts back pen)*

SGT KAY   So you're not a practising physician, you are in
administrator.

DR KOLA   Yes.

SGT KAY   Good, let's talk about your administering.

DR KOLA   Excuse me, do you mind if I relieve myself? I've been
suffering from a rather weak bladder of late.

SGT KAY   Be my guest.

Dr Kola uses the bucket provided by the prison. He turns his back to audience.

DR KOLA   *(Much relieved)* Thank you.

SGT KAY   Not at all. You say you are an administrator and that you are no longer a physician?

DR KOLA   Yes, you've asked me that.

SGT KAY   But yet there is one patient you dealt with.

DR KOLA   I beg your pardon?

SGT KAY   Didn't you used to treat the Chief Minister?

DR KOLA   Well, the Chief Minister, what can I say? He was an exception, he was not a patient as such.

SGT KAY   What was he, a friend? Would you call him a friend, Doctor?

DR KOLA   Well, something less than a friend, certainly. After all, I was never one to be known socially with him.

SGT KAY   Were you not his personal physician?

DR KOLA   Well . . . not really, he had his physicians in London.

SGT KAY   Were you not called upon to treat him for fatigue?

DR KOLA   I may have been asked to advise –

SGT KAY   Didn't you treat him for syphilis?

DR KOLA   *(Leaping to his feet)* My god!

SGT KAY   What's the matter, Doctor, your bladder again?

DR KOLA   Your information is rather –

SGT KAY   Accurate.

DR KOLA   *(Sitting down again)* That's not quite the word I would have used. Inflammatory, I would have said.

SGT KAY   True. Every word. How many times were you called upon to perform operations on girls that he'd gotten –

DR KOLA   I merely supervised, I myself never performed a gynaecological operation.

SGT KAY   It was your discretion which was so valuable to him, wasn't it, Doctor?

DR KOLA   He confided in me . . . when he chose to.

SGT KAY   And he rewarded your discretion with a cabinet post.

DR KOLA   I take offence at that statement.

SGT KAY   You are not in a position to take offence at a goddamn thing, Doctor.

DR KOLA   All right, you have me –

SGT KAY   By the balls, so please don't make me have to squeeze them. We know what went on in the prison interrogation centre.

DR KOLA   You have me at your mercy but still I must say this: it was not because of my duplicity that I was given a position but because of my competence.

SGT KAY   Yes, well, let's deal with your competence. It was in 1970 that the hospital began construction?

DR KOLA   Do you know how hard I worked for that hospital to be finally approved?

SGT KAY   Construction was finally completed in 1975.

DR KOLA   Yes, it was a very slow and difficult process.

SGT KAY   Now we have a hospital and nothing in it.

DR KOLA   Just let me say that it is not may fault –

SGT KAY   You are head of the Ministry of Health?

DR KOLA   Month after month I have been trying to get the Chief Minister to deal with that problem.

SGT KAY   He was too busy dealing with alcohol and syphilis, too busy crushing students, finding out where and who the opponents were. Too busy running to Europe chasing your wife.

DR KOLA   *(Leaping to his feet again)* What?

SGT KAY   Yes, the good Chief Minister was too busy in his affairs to see about the hospital. He had to make certain that when the people cried for more rice they were shot down in the street. He was too busy seeing that the unions would not organize and cause him further embarrassment in America.

DR KOLA   That bitch, I'll kill her.

SGT KAY   That's all you care about, the betrayal of one woman's body. Meanwhile three-quarters of the country is on the starvation line.

DR KOLA   Of course I care about the people. Do you know how many papers I've published on the problems of rural disease?

SGT KAY   It's too bad the people couldn't eat your papers. *(He reads aloud)* 'Food is a political commodity. The best we can try and do is to feed the starving who are themselves only children of the poor.' Very eloquent.

DR KOLA   What more could I do? Could I kill? I'm a doctor, not a soldier.

SGT KAY   But you have killed, you've helped kill.

DR KOLA   I may have helped kill but I myself have not killed. If any died it was without my knowledge.

SGT KAY   Without your knowledge? Do you know that over half of Africa is under fourteen? What chance if they don't eat?

What good if the market is full and there is no money to buy?

DR KOLA   I agree.

SGT KAY   Of course you agree, as long as your belly is full. The middle class like you could buy at half price, while we who grew it could not even afford to eat it. Is that freedom?

DR KOLA   It is not me you should be asking, it is the Chief Minister.

SGT KAY   We would have asked him but a bullet put paid to all questions. So that only leaves you, Doctor.

DR KOLA   Am I any more guilty than any of the others?

SGT KAY   Are you any less guilty?

DR KOLA   Yes. I at least tried. The others just wanted to stay in power. I am like you, I come from the village, from the bush.

SGT KAY   That only makes you *more* guilty.

DR KOLA   And so now you feel you can put it all right.

SGT KAY   I think I could do no worse than your generation.

DR KOLA   Really, you think not? When they're ready for you God himself can't help you.

SGT KAY   You're such a religious man, Dr Kola, tell me, if Christ came back today, what do you think he would do?

DR KOLA   If Christ came back today they would crucify him, only quicker.

SGT KAY   But if he were to come, what form do you think he would take?

DR KOLA   What do you think? A soldier, of course.

SGT KAY   Yes, I think he would have to come back as a soldier, especially in Africa.

DR KOLA   Riding a tank, no doubt.

SGT KAY   If necessary, yes. My parents wanted me to be a doctor but after seeing you I no longer wanted to be a doctor.

DR KOLA   It's easy to judge when you're in power, but I would like to see what happens when you find out that a gun is not enough to stabilize Africa. War is not enough. A state of emergency is not enough.

SGT KAY   A pity you never told your Chief Minister that.

DR KOLA   I tried to.

SGT KAY   Do you know what my father said to me on his death bed? He said, 'Son, I would have liked you to go to university. I would have liked to know that my son went to university. But I would rather know that my son is alive. And so, if you must be a soldier in order to live, then be a soldier, for to be a soldier is not necessarily a bad thing' My father fought in the war and through it he got to see the white man for the first time as what he really was. Before that he thought they were invincible, but through the war he saw that they are just men like other men. As frightened to die as other men and just as capable of killing their brothers and more so. Before that, he thought that they only killed Africans.

DR KOLA   All of that is very interesting, but what exactly do you intend to do with me?

SGT KAY   There are still a number of questions that have to be answered. For example, what happened to all of that money which was allocated for the hospital?

DR KOLA   I have no idea.

SGT KAY   You'll have to do better than that.

DR KOLA   I can't do any better, I never saw any money.

SGT KAY   So where did it go?

DR KOLA   You'll have to ask the Minister of Finance.

SGT KAY   I did ask him.

DR KOLA   And so?

SGT KAY   He said I should ask you.

DR KOLA   The bastard.

SGT KAY   Those are your associates.

DR KOLA   I know nothing of any money.

SGY KAY   Then you were badly deceived. The hospital was poorly built and all that money for modern equipment somehow vanished into people's accounts in London and Switzerland. Do you have a Swiss account, Doctor?

DR KOLA   Well, yes . . . for my family, but I can assure you I have no more than anyone else. Have you checked the Chief Minister's accounts?

SGT KAY   Yes we have, Doctor. *(Closes file and stands)* Thank you. Goodbye.

DR KOLA   You don't understand. I merely tried to take care of my family. Everyone in the government was corrupt. You can't keep beating your head against a wall. What will you do with me?

SGT KAY   We'll come for you some morning at dawn. At a time of our choosing. Until then you wait, as we waited.

DR KOLA   Wait? I would prefer to take my own life. If you could just bring me my valise I would be obliged.

SGT KAY   I'm afraid not.

DR KOLA   Look, what difference does it make how I die? Surely the important thing is –

SGT KAY   If the Chief Minister had taken me prisoner, he would not have let me choose my death.

DR KOLA   *(Taking off watch)* Here, this is a Rolex watch, do you
    know how much it's worth?

SGT KAY   Not enough, Doctor, not enough to save your life.

DR KOLA   I have money.

SGT KAY   Oh yes, we know you have money. Tell me, Doctor, if it
    were not for the fact that you people had the money to go
    abroad so easily whenever you felt ill, don't you think that
    the hospital here would have been built a long, long time
    ago?

DR KOLA   That may be, God knows I tried my best but . . . well,
    I'm not speaking of hospitals now. I'm speaking of money
    which you will have use for, coup or no coup.

SGT KAY   We thought of holding you prisoner and getting your
    wife to withdraw money from your account in exchange.

DR KOLA   Yes, contact her, she could see to it.

SGT KAY   I'm afraid that she doesn't have the slightest reason for
    keeping you alive. You see, in your attempt to provide
    security for your family, you signed your own death warrant.

DR KOLA   The bitch would let me die?

SGT KAY   I'm afraid so. You are no further use to her, *(Pause)*
    and you were never any use to us. You are not the solution,
    you are the problem.

DR KOLA   You will need a physician.

SGT KAY   Yes, but I'm afraid I could never really trust you.

DR KOLA   *(Grabbing the sergeant's arm)* But there are things
    I could tell you.

SGT KAY   Nothing which we don't already know. Goodbye, Dr
    Kola. Read your Bible.

    He exits

DR KOLA   *(Takes Bible and flings it to the floor)* Come back,
bring me my valise. Please. There are some pills I need to
take. Please don't leave me. *(He begins to vomit into the
bucket which he had urinated into earlier)* Soon it will be
your turn. *(Sits on the floor and begins to rock)* I could be
very valuable to you. I'm a graduate of . . . You don't have
to kill me . . . It really makes no sense, I'm no threat to
anyone. If you just let me go away . . . quietly. You see, I'm
not a well man. I . . . have a family. *(He looks up and sees
overhanging bar – he takes a stool and stands on it, using
his silk tie as a noose – he tests it for strength and then
thinks better of it)* No! What a waste of a perfectly good silk
tie. *(Steps down from stool)* Yesterday, they didn't even
know how to use a toilet. They were still wiping their
bottoms with leaves. Now they want to rule the country –
Fools! What right have you to judge me? Who was your
father's father's father? You think running a country is easy,
just like a stall in a market? Go on, my friend. Rule!

There is a lighting change to suggest a change of time.

*Sits on stool thinking for a while and then begins to pace
slowly and a bit awkwardly at first – awkward such as a man
is before his son.*

DR KOLA   My dear son
Perhaps . . . perhaps by the time you receive this letter, I will
be dead.
They have not told me either the time or the manner of my
execution. They have merely told me that it will come. I can
only tell you as my father told me: 'The sentence of life is
death.' Be certain of one thing, my son. That I will not have
taken my own life.
It is not in me to do such a thing.
Pause
In a way they have done me some service by this sentence.
I've had some time to read and think.
Who in Africa has time to read or think? Only students, and

only because they must. As for the rest of us, once the degrees are gotten we're much too busy jumping into bed with other men's wives to read. Too busy with intrigues, alliances and scandals and all the other rituals of civilization.

Pause

If you sleep with a whore, you must expect to wake with sores. I am not a child, I must take the weight of manhood and not jump the knife. What I did I thought I was doing for my family – now I don't know.

You, my son, are in America,

my wife is in England,

my daughter in Europe,

and yet which of you will weep for your father?

Which of you will weep for your husband?

And when you hear the word 'COUNTRY' which of you will think of Africa?

He laughs in self mockery and then suddenly changes mood

And yet I use the word 'family'.

Pause

I don't envy you your youth.

I don't envy you America or England or Europe or the whole western world.

I don't . . . I don't envy you.

When I was young the way you are young, I wanted to be a doctor but now is not the time of doctors, now is the time of soldiers.

Even under sentence of death as I am, I prefer this madness to that one. I would rather die in Africa than be a joke in Europe.

I'm sorry that's the way of it.

One last thing I ask of you.

Pause

If you cannot bring yourself to come home, at least do this for me. Do not marry one of them. All right, if you must live among them, live;

Pause
but do not marry.
If you marry, no child . . . no child.
Please do not divide the tribe any more than it already is.
Your mother may not mind dying among the English . . . I
do.
I'm at peace. I know my guilt.
Not that I was a thief
but that I moved among thieves.
Not that I was a louse
but that I saw the sucking of blood and said nothing.
Tell me this, my son, who is it who wins in the world –
those who stay or those who flee?
And what is winning if to win is to become a beast
Pause
like the others?

The stage darkens as Sergeant Kay enters the cell

And this too you will come to know.

Darkness.

THAT GENERATION

CAST
Wallace
Phyllis (Mrs Wallace)
Carol

Setting: A furnished room in Shepherds Bush, London

Wallace, early forties, hair parted in middle, moves in the manner of an old cricketer.

SCENE I

Music: Thelonius Monk, 'I'm Confessing'

*Wallace, dressed in long underwear, a scarf and jacket, no trousers.
Busy boiling egg. Location: furnished room, West London. Time: late
Fifties.*

WALLACE   Being a failure isn't easy. It takes application at first,
stick-to itness. After a while you get the hang of it, then it's
all clear sailing. The nice thing about failure is that people
leave you the hell alone. No phone calls in the middle of
the night. No big set of party and thing. Just quiet. *(Checks
egg to see if it's hard yet – burns fingers)* When I first started
to work for London Transport I felt like I was coming down
in the world but soon I learn that nobody really sees you
when you're wearing a uniform. It's just like carnival,
everybody dress up in their dreams. Of course, being a
failure is harder when you used to have money, but after a
time you get used to the sacred embrace of poverty, it
clutches you right around the bollocks.

*Sound of footsteps, someone pushes envelope under door,
Wallace looks terrified.*

Oh Jesus, what's this now! *(Picks up envelope haltingly and
reads with shaking hand)* Dear Wallace, will arrive London
Friday the thirteenth, one pm. Boat train. Love, Phyllis.

Darkness

SCENE II

*Lights up on Victoria Station where Wallace has just arrived to meet
Phyllis.*

WALLACE   God, I would be late. Had to fix the place up for her.
Couldn't bring her back to that mess; never hear the end of
it. Had to take the day off. Lose a day's pay. It's starting

already, she is costing me money. Where the hell is she? Hardly remember what she looks like. I wonder if she's gotten fat. Five years. No, she wouldn't have . . . always takes pride in the way . . . My God, there she is. Wave Wallace. That's it, lift your hand. Try to look happy.

Phyllis?

PHYLLIS   Oh God, Wallace. Hold me no. It's so long I haven't seen you. You still part your hair in the middle. You all right? I was afraid the telegram didn't reach you. *(Excited)* Oh God, Wallace.

WALLACE   I'm sorry I'm a little late. Did you have to wait long?

PHYLLIS   No, I was talking to this girl She's from San Fernando. Come meet her. But why you walking so; something wrong with your foot?

WALLACE   It's nothing, it comes and goes.

PHYLLIS   Wallace, this is Carol. Carol, my husband Wallace.

CAROL   *(Shy)* Please to meet you.

WALLACE   Nice to meet you, Carol.

PHYLLIS   Girl, you not cold, you don't have no coat. This not Trinidad, you know.

CAROL   *(Trying to pretend she's not freezing)* No, I'm all right. Soon as my friend Peter comes he'll bring some things for me.

PHYLLIS   You're sure he's going to meet you?

CAROL   Oh yes, I write him and tell him for meet me here.

PHYLLIS   You have money?

CAROL   I have sufficient.

PHYLLIS   Wallace, what you think?

WALLACE   I'm sure she'll be all right. Where are your things, Phyllis?

PHYLLIS   These three suitcases and that trunk and that box there. Everything on that cart.

WALLACE   Good God, all that's yours!

PHYLLIS   How you mean, I just bring these few things them. I left everything to ship over. *(To Carol)* Listen girl, you better hold this sweater.

CAROL   Oh no, I couldn't take it.

PHYLLIS   Go on, you go catch your death in that thin dress you're wearing. And here, you better take this shawl too.

CAROL   I'm sure Peter is going to come just now.

PHYLLIS   Well, if he doesn't come, do you have any place to stay?

CAROL   Oh, I have an aunt here.

WALLACE   Phyllis, we better get started. I can't see us taking all this on a bus.

PHYLLIS   Bus, what bus? That's what they have taxi for.

CAROL   Please give me your address so I can return these things to you.

PHYLLIS   My husband will write it for you. Wallace?

WALLACE   Yes Phyllis, of course. You have a piece of paper?

CAROL   Here, use the inside of this Bible.

WALLACE   Oh yes, they always give you a Bible to travel with, don't they?

CAROL   *(Laughs)* Yes, it was my Mother's

WALLACE   Here you are.

CAROL   Thank you so much.

WALLACE   Well, all the best. Goodbye.

CAROL   Goodbye.

PHYLLIS   Goodbye. Walk good. *(She kisses Carol and then whispers)* And hold on to this, find yourself a room if he don't come. Go on take it.

CAROL   God bless you.

WALLACE   What did you do, give her money beside?

PHYLLIS   Can't just leave her so in a strange place.

WALLACE   So who you is, Rockerfeller? You can't be so kind in this place, Phyllis. This not back home. Here everyone looking for a freeness, you understand. They'll suck you dry if you let them.

PHYLLIS   Wallace that's not like you. You were always good to people. How you turn so hard?

WALLACE   England is hard Phyllis. Well let's see about this taxi. You know how much it's going to cost, at least twlve shillings and he'll be expecting a tip with this load.

PHYLLIS   You glad to see me or you're not glad to see me?

WALLACE   Of course I'm glad.

PHYLLIS   Well you don't show it.

WALLACE   I'm sorry. *(He kisses her).*

PHYLLIS   You don't even ask after the children.

WALLACE   Give me a chance. My head spinning. Come let we go home. Taxi, taxi.

   Darkness.

SCENE III

Returning with wife

WALLACE   Just a minute, I'll get this door open. *(Straining with suitcase)* Right, here we are. I'm sorry it's so high up. I'll take that.

PHYLLIS   My God, you didn't tell me it was the top floor.

WALLACE   Well, at least it's not so noisy up here. You don't have to hear the traffic. Well, this is it. The bath is the second door on the right and the toilet is at the end of the hall.

PHYLLIS   You mean we have to share it?

WALLACE   The fellow downstairs drives a lorry. He's almost never home and seldom bathes. It won't be so bad. Take off you things. Let me move these things so you can sit down. *(Shifts newspapers)*

PHYLLIS   You mean to tell me that all you have is a room?

WALLACE   Well, accommodations are hard to find in London.

PHYLLIS   This is what you left home for?

WALLACE   Please.

PHYLLIS   Well, where am I suppose to stay?

WALLACE   I've thrown out a lot of old things. I've made some room in the closet for you dresses.

PHYLLIS   I can't believe it. At home we had a twelve-room house, Wallace.

WALLACE   This is not back home, Phyllis.

PHYLLIS   But why, I can't understand. Why would you live here? My God, it's just a –

WALLACE   Room, Phyllis, just a room, but at least we have some privacy.

PHYLLIS Privacy, what privacy? You knew I was coming, the least you could have done was get a decent place.

WALLACE I never asked you to come. It was you who wrote and said you were coming. I told you not to expect anything good.

PHYLLIS I didn't expect anything good, but a room, a furnished room, Wallace. What have you come to?

WALLACE England, that's what I've come to.

PHYLLIS At home you had your own business, two cars, a house. What do you have here?

WALLACE A job and peace and quiet, or at least I did until now. *(Takes a drink of Mt Gay rum)* Did you bring me some rum?

PHYLLIS Yes, I bring four bottles. They gave me some trouble at Customs, but I got through.

WALLACE Thank God for that. It's a long time since I drank some decent liquor.

PHYLLIS Jesus Mary and Joseph, look at those curtains on the window. Where you find these things, boy?

WALLACE These are the landlady's prize possessions.

PHYLLIS Prize possession, they're just good to burn. Look at this furniture.

WALLACE After a while you get use to it.

PHYLLIS I would never get use to this. But you not shame to bring people here? What your friends must think?

WALLACE I have few friends that come here.

PHYLLIS Why were you so late to come and pick me up?

WALLACE I told you, there was a mix-up at the pier. The boat train was early.

PHYLLIS   I thought you weren't coming again.

WALLACE   You knew I'd come.

PHYLLIS   I don't know anything. You've changed, Wallace.

WALLACE   Well, you haven't changed at all.

PHYLLIS   All these years and you didn't send for me.

WALLACE   You were doing all right. Certainly better than I was.

PHYLLIS   You could still have sent for me.

WALLACE   I would have preferred to have something better to
       show you.

PHYLLIS   You working?

WALLACE   Well, London Transport.

PHYLLIS   What that is?

WALLACE   I collect tickets. I'm a ticket collector.

PHYLLIS   A ticket collector?

WALLACE   It's a job. There's a chance of promotion to inspector.

PHYLLIS   You still play cricket?

WALLACE   When I can on Sunday. When I'm not too tired.

PHYLLIS   You could have been like Constantine or any of them.

WALLACE   Could have been.

PHYLLIS   I don't understand.

WALLACE   Will you stop saying you don't understand.

PHYLLIS   *(Starting to clear up room)* Well, what do you intend to
       do?

WALLACE   I don't know, many things go through my mind.
       Maybe I'll win the pools.

PHYLLIS A ticket collector, with all the qualifications you have.

WALLACE When I first came, I used to write down all my
qualifications.

PHYLLIS Did you tell them all the positions which you've held?

WALLACE I told them, and do you know what they said? They
said I was in a rare category. They said I was an over-skilled
coloured. I was too qualified for anything they had to offer.
So finally I learned to stop giving all my qualifications when
I went for an interview. They don't like it here. They feel
that you're putting on airs.

PHYLLIS You're just telling the truth.

WALLACE The truth is that over-qualified and under-qualified,
you end up in the same position: *unemployed*, that's the
truth.

PHYLLIS Then this country is a damn waste then.

WALLACE You take what you can get. London Transport or
nothing.

PHYLLIS You could have come back home.

WALLACE Back home to what? Gossip, scandal, cliques of
power, affairs and the same faces.

PHYLLIS Aunt Anne send a cake for you.

WALLACE Good.

PHYLLIS And Joe send two manoges. They're well ripe. Joe want
to know why you haven't written.

WALLACE To say what? Having wonderful time, wish you were
here?

PHYLLIS Everyone expected –

WALLACE To hear great things. That I had passed the bar exams

and was some big solicitor? Well, it didn't happen. Nothing
happen, just time and rent.

PHYLLIS   Where you cook? I don't see any kitchen.

WALLACE   I use the hotplate there in the corner.

PHYLLIS   Hotplate?

WALLACE   An electric fire.

PHYLLIS   My God! So what you does eat, Wallace?

WALLACE   Well, I usually cook a large pot of rice and peas on
Sunday and make do for the rest of the week.

PHYLLIS   You rather do this than come home where you have
family and friends? Look outside there, all you could see is
rain. You not seeing nothing. Is this life at all?

WALLACE   You get use to it.

PHYLLIS   You just shut yourself up in here because you too
shame to go home?

WALLACE   Well, one thing about failure, at least it's private.

PHYLLIS   So is death. *(After a beat)* Where you say the toilet is
again?

WALLACE   In the hall.

PHYLLIS   I dread to use it, but I can't hold out no longer.

WALLACE   The spirit is willing but the flesh is weak. Here you
better take my bathrobe.

PHYLLIS   Thanks. I don't plan on making a holiday of it.

WALLACE   First door on your right. And be careful for the
doorknob. *(Phyllis exists)*

God, I know what she's feeling. Her first English winter. The
sky's grey and the streets grey. And the houses all look so
alike, repeating themselves like a child's maths. But did

they never tell you about this city of deception, where men go with their heels broken down and their souls broken down. This place where people search for little corners of darkness to hide in – and wait.

Music fades in for flashback to a Sunday in Trinidad. The sound of calypso: 'Cricket Lovely Cricket!'

PHYLLIS   *(Entering from church)* Wallace you awake?

WALLACE   *(Grunting)* Well I am now. What time is it?

PHYLLIS   It's three o'clock in the afternoon. I've just come from church. It was a beautiful service. You must come next Sunday.

WALLACE   Me, no thanks, I've had enough of church to last me until my funeral.

PHYLLIS   Don't blaspheme. You want to eat? The maid is off today but she left something there I could heat up. You really must talk to her you know, she's getting quite beside herself.

WALLACE   What's the matter with Katie now?

PHYLLIS   She wants every Sunday off now. I don't know what she expects us to do for supper. We can't even have company come anymore. Sometimes I have to ask myself which one is suppose to be the servant. She's getting too familiar.

WALLACE   I'll have to talk with her.

PHYLLIS   Your eyes are all bloodshot, Wallace. You've been up playing cards all night again.

WALLACE   And so?

PHYLLIS   Why don't you ever come home on a weekend? Don't you think the children would like to spend some time with you? You could go to church with us one Sunday at least.

WALLACE   The church is everything to you, isn't it Phyllis? Is it the church or the gossiping. Suppose you had to give up everything. Blessed are the poor for they shall be called what? The children of God, isnt it? Suppose you became poor, Phyllis.

PHYLLIS   I think I could stand it.

WALLACE   *(Taunting)* Oh really, you would give up everything.

PHYLLIS   Yes, if I had to.

WALLACE   Give up the maids and the house and the two cars and the driveway and the garden you love so much?

PHYLLIS   Yes.

WALLACE   And the parties and receptions and the society gossip. You wouldn't mind giving all that up? Well you may soon have your chance to find out.

PHYLLIS   Is what you mean, find out?

WALLACE   I'm selling the business. ·

PHYLLIS   Selling the business?

WALLACE   Yes, selling the refinery. Lock stock and barrel. Everything one time. Bam, just like that.

PHYLLIS   I don't understand. Is joke you making?

WALLACE   I know you don't understand. You never did.

PHYLLIS   *(Excited)* Well explain yourself no. Don't just treat me like I'm some little fool you're trifling with. Why do you want to sell off the business?

WALLACE   Because it makes me sick, that's why. It's not what I want to do.

PHYLLIS   Well, I never know that's not what you want. You never said anything before.

WALLACE   Of course I have. Everyday I tell you how bored I am with it all. Sometimes I just wish the whole damn thing would burn down and this island with it.

PHYLLIS   Well, I hear you complain sometimes, but I never know you were so serious.

WALLACE   This island is suffocating me. I feel like I'm choking to death. And no one understands.

PHYLLIS   But Wallace, you've got everything a man could want. Money, position, family. What more . . .

WALLACE   All the time I'm doing what everyone else wants. When do I start to do what I want? I never wanted to marry, you know, Phyllis. The family kept after me, wearing me down. 'It's time, you know Wallace. You have to settle down and act sensible. You can't just run the streets'. All right, so I married. Then you wanted us to move here. We have to keep up appearances. Bigger houses, more property. Keep moving every two years. I was content to live right there in my father's house. We could have added on an extension. It was fine. A good house, sturdy and simple. My history is there in that house. But no, you wouldn't have it.

PHYLLIS   I'm sorry, your mother never liked me, and I refuse to live under her will. You're not a child, why should we stay in their house?

WALLACE   Because that's the way *we* do things.

PHYLLIS   Well that's not the way I do things. We would never have had a moment's peace there. I wouldn't have anyway. *(Pause)* Listen, it's Sunday, I don't want to argue, the neighbours will hear us.

WALLACE   So what if it's Sunday. Sunday is a good day for truth, isn't it?

PHYLLIS   Wallace, the neighbours are home.

WALLACE   To hell with the neighbours. What are they, just a
          bunch of rich Assyrian Jews. Their money is no better than
          mine. You think I care if they hear me? If I was poor they
          wouldn't even spit on me. That's the way things are on this
          island, lies and more lies. Hatred and scandal with only
          greed holding it all together. To hell with the neighbours. If
          I want to stand up in the middle of Frederick Street and
          cuss, I will. To hell with the neighbours.

PHYLLIS   This isn't a barracks yard you know, Wallace. You not
          dealing with one of your cheap Jamette girls.

WALLACE   You know what's wrong with you Phyllis, you're just
          like the island. You suffocate.

PHYLLIS   I suffocate you? I never made you do anything. I never
          beg you to marry me. I never force you to move here. It's
          you who is always trying to measure up to your brothers. It's
          you who is always bringing up the fact that they're
          barristers, and how high up they are in the government. It's
          you who feels inferior.

WALLACE   Inferior. Me feel inferior? You must be mad. What
          have they got that I want? I make as much money as them,
          more in fact. What have they got?

PHYLLIS   Degrees, Wallace. Degrees. That's what's eating you up.

WALLACE   That's a damn lie.

PHYLLIS   Is it. Is it Wallace?

WALLACE   This place is just misery.

PHYLLIS   Where you going?

WALLACE   Out to get drunk. What else to do on your glorious
          Trinidad Sunday? (Slams door. Music of calypso builds up
          as Phyllis calls after him.)

          Present time

WALLACE   *(Talking to himself)* You never really understood, did you Phyllis?

(Sound of banging on a distant door followed by muffled screams)

PHYLLIS   *(Offstage)* Wallace, Wallace!

WALLACE   Oh my God, it's Phyllis. *(Calls)* Phyllis, what's wrong?

PHYLLIS   The door won't open.

WALLACE   *(Runs off stage)* Hold on. Oh damn, the knob come off. Be calm Wallace, be calm. Um . . . Phyllis, can you turn the knob from your side?

PHYLLIS   It's come off in my hand.

WALLACE   Oh, well listen, I can't do anything from my side. You'll have to push the knob from your side through on your end and I'll push on mine, okay?

PHYLLIS   Jesus, what a place to come to die. *(Sound of fumbling)* All right I'll push it back in. Hurry up, it's freezing in here.

WALLACE   Okay now, turn to the right, that's it, now push. *(Sound of lock catching and opening)* There we are. Hello.

Enter Phyllis and Wallace.

PHYLLIS   Jesus Mary and Joseph. You take this thing for joke. I thought I was going dead in there. *(She kisses him)*

WALLACE   Come on by the electric fire.

PHYLLIS   Wallace, you mean to say people really pay rent to live in something like this?

WALLACE   Two pounds five a week, Phyllis.

PHYLLIS   But how people could live so?

WALLACE   With difficulty Phyllis, with difficulty.

Darkness.

SCENE IV

The same room the following morning. Wallace getting ready for work. Sitting at table finishing coffee.

WALLACE   God, Phyllis, I haven't had a breakfast like that in years. I feel like going back to bed. How do you expect man to work after a breakfast like that?

PHYLLIS   Well, you didn't get much sleep last night.

WALLACE   *(Laughing contentedly)* And whose fault was that?

PHYLLIS   Wallace. You can't take the day off? Dou dou, darling.

WALLACE   I already took yesterday off. London Transport isn't a hobby you know, it's a job.

PHYLLIS   All right then.

WALLACE   Don't worry *(Kisses her)* we'll have a bit of time to catch up.

PHYLLIS   Wallace, you remember this dress?

WALLACE   Which dress you talking?

PHYLLIS   This white one.

WALLACE   You still have that.

PHYLLIS   You use to say it was your favourite.

WALLACE   Did I?

PHYLLIS   Yes. I wore it the day we first met.

WALLACE   *(Upset)* I . . . can't remember. That was a long time ago.

Flashback. Music: 'I'm Confessing'.

Wallace appearing in gleaming white shirt and trousers of the cricketer. He stretches forth his hand and is met by the image of his wife Phyllis as a young debutante in Trinidad.

WALLACE   *(Musing)* And at that time I was Queen's Royal
      College and you were convent school and all full of Mass
      and tea and Latin. Garden parties and beatitudes. And I . . .
      I was cricket and English history. It took several generations
      to form you. Just the right skin colour, just the right mixture
      of East and West. The pain of the plantation had left your
      eyes and now the certainty of certainty was there.

      (Normal voice) Hello Miss Phyllis Bacchus, I hope you
      won't think me forward if I say I find you beautiful.

PHYLLIS   Not at all, although perhaps I should, we've not been
      introduced.

WALLACE   But you know me.

PHYLLIS   *(Holding Chinese fan)* I've seen you about.

WALLACE   *(Musing)* And so we played the game together and
      after six months we were seen in public places. I talked
      cricket with your father and never politics. *(They dance
      together to the music of 'I'm Confessing'. They dance
      slowly and beautifully. He comes forward, leaving her in
      background)* We spoke of Frank Worrell and Constantine.
      The new age of cricketers. I was going to be like them. No
      more black bowler, white batsman. But you were so beauti-
      ful, Phyllis, why didn't I leave you just so? A nice, useless
      debutante who didn't even know how to boil water. But
      instead I married you, or did you marry me?

      Back to present.

PHYLLIS   I knew that you had made a baby with that coolie girl in
      San Fernando.

WALLACE   You knew before we were married?

PHYLLIS   Of course I knew. My mother held it against you, but I
      told her that a lot of other men had done the same thing.
      You see, I thought you would change, Wallace. I should
      have known – well no matter, I was very young, you see.

WALLACE   What else was there to do back home? What else
        beside women, cricket, drink and gamble? After all, we had
        more than enough of everything. Money was no problem.
        Boredom was the only problem. How to stop yourself from
        thinking. Those who have can do what they want and those
        who don't, well they do what they can. We just had too
        much. Too much sun. Too much food. Too much wealth.
        Too much everything.

PHYLLIS   And so why did you bother to marry me?

WALLACE   There were girls you stroked and girls you married.
        My family liked you.

PHYLLIS   And after we were married, and after you locked me up
        safely in the big new house, you never bothered to come
        home.

WALLACE   I came home. *(Pause)* at first.

PHYLLIS   To sleep and change your clothes. It started that
        Carnival week, you got drunk and you stayed drunk. Out
        every night, but I couldn't go anywhere.

WALLACE   I'm my father's son. He never let my mother go out.

PHYLLIS   So I must stay home like one of your cricket trophies, to
        be shown to friends and then put away.

WALLACE   You wanted children, I gave them to you.

PHYLLIS   That wasn't enough.

WALLACE   I did what I thought was right.

PHYLLIS   And all those women?

WALLACE   Whatever women I had I needed at the time.

PHYLLIS   You needed them for what?

WALLACE   To forget. Sugar and rum is what born us. It's planta-
        tion we come from, girl, and then we try and put on the
        face of England on top of it. It's like we're always playing

Mas. It can drive you mad.

PHYLLIS   And so one day you just up and sell the business. You don't discuss anything with me or anybody. You just sell off everything and say you're going away. No explanation, no reason.

WALLACE   I just couldn't take anymore.

PHYLLIS   You had things so easy.

WALLACE   Too easy.

PHYLLIS   You mother said you were mad. There was always madness somewhere in you.

WALLACE   One day I looked at my friends, I looked at myself. We were young, we were successful and we were dead. We shared the same parties, we shared the same women, we went to the same schools. Some went into politics, some went into the civil service, some went into their father's business. It's like stealing a car on the island. Where could you go with it except into the sea?

PHYLLIS   And so you just ran away and left us.

WALLACE   I left you money.

PHYLLIS   Money wasn't enough. How long do you think it was before the vultures came? What could I tell them except that you were sending for us? But how long would they believe that? One year, two?

WALLACE   You had family, you could make a life.

PHYLLIS   What life?

WALLACE   I couldn't . . . I tried to keep the lie going. Keep the smile, keep the drinks flowing, but I couldn't.

PHYLLIS   At first I thought you might have come back.

WALLACE   If I could come in disguise and just sit and watch the sea; go in the cocoa fields and pass for someone else.

PHYLLIS   You talk as if you kill someone. There's no one hunting for you.

WALLACE   But I did kill someone, Phyllis.

PHYLLIS   What you talking? You kill someone?

WALLACE   The Wallace they thought they knew so well. The Wallace they could always come to lend money from. The Wallace that was always good for a fete.

PHYLLIS   Again when your friends realized you weren't coming again, you should have seen them, boy. Oh God, night and day they coming. Friends for so.

WALLACE   They always wanted you.

PHYLLIS   First they tried politics – 'Phyllis, if you ever need a friend in high places, don't fear to call on me. Wallace and me were like brothers from small . . .' Then when I didn't come . . .

WALLACE   They wanted to service you.

PHYLLIS   They made sure that my life was hard. They wanted me to beg.

WALLACE   But you had money.

PHYLLIS   Money doesn't last forever, you know.

WALLACE   You were always ambitious, Phyllis.

PHYLLIS   Why, because I wanted to keep my head up? I was never cheap, Wallace, I wasn't raised that way. You wanted your two children to look as if dog eat they supper?

WALLACE   They still call Paul the little prince, don't they?

PHYLLIS   You don't care that he doesn't know his father. He could never love you now.

WALLACE   My father stayed home all the time I was growing up and I still have no love for him. What's the difference?

Would it be better that I stayed and died from a stomach ulcer? So they could say Wallace was a good 'Tess'?

PHYLLIS   But, Wallace, tell me good so I could understand, you feel is we who cause you to drink?

WALLACE   I'm not saying you cause me to drink. What I'm saying is that the only way I could stand home was to drink. Not just you, all of it. I have to get dressed for work.

PHYLLIS   And there where there was a brighter sun.

WALLACE   To here where there is no sun.

PHYLLIS   In the mornings you could wake and smell the cocoa in the fields. What you could smell here, Wallace?

WALLACE   Piss and death.

PHYLLIS   So why –

WALLACE   Look, I have to go to work, Phyllis.

PHYLLIS   You look so funny in that uniform, that's not you, Wallace.

WALLACE   No, Phyllis, it's not me.

PHYLLIS   So why we don't just leave.
Let them keep they job.
Let them keep they England.
Come no man.

Holding him

WALLACE   I can't go back.

PHYLLIS   But is what the ass wrong with you. You mean to dead here?

WALLACE   I'll . . . be late.

PHYLLIS   You 'fraid.

WALLACE   Cricket makes sense. You bowl line and length, line

and length, eventually you get a man out. But life, life is
different. Is the thing you love which kills you, the place you
live which crushes you, and there is no sense. Here at least
no one knows you.

PHYLLIS   And so it's good that no one knows you?

WALLACE   Look, I'm going to be late for work.

PHYLLIS   Give me those shoes. *(She starts to brush them off)*
When a man looks bad, his woman also looks bad.

WALLACE   You know they call me Captain.

PHYLLIS   So why they call you Captain?

WALLACE   Just a name they give me.

PHYLLIS   Well, it sounds very forward to me. Like they making
sport of you. Tell them your name is not Captain, it's Mr.
Wallace.

WALLACE   *(Taking shoes)* Thank you. What that calypso you
used to sing? *(He hums it)*

PHYLLIS   'Take me, take me, I am feeling lonely
Take me down some lonesome road
but don't make me mother know'.

WALLACE   That's the one. *(He kisses her)* You'll be here when I
come? It will be about ten.

PHYLLIS   Where I'm going?

WALLACE   See you

He exits, singing calypso

PHYLLIS   *(Looking about room)* Well, Great Britain, you not so
great now, Still, you'll have to do until we can do better.
(Pause) Lord, please don't let this man die here in
England. Please Father. I'll make a go of it and try again
with him. If it must be here, well so be it, but please Lord let

us die where we were born, not here among strangers. *(A knock is heard at door)* Wallace is that you?

VOICE   Hello, is Phyllis there?

PHYLLIS   Oh Carol, how you doing girl?

CAROL   I bring back your sweater for you. I can't stop. *(She takes off her things and pushes her way in.)*

PHYLLIS   Oh bless you. You didn't have to rush. You find your way all right, your fellow come for you?

CAROL   Peter, yes he come finally. I was well-vex with him.

PHYLLIS   Come in no, I'm sorry for the state of the place, I haven't a chance to really do much. We won't be staying here much longer.

CAROL   Don't bother to explain, the place we're staying is even smaller. Two of us can't even dress at the same time.

PHYLLIS   Will you have some tea? Let me just put the kettle on.

CAROL   Don't put yourself to any trouble.

PHYLLIS   No trouble, I was just going to have some.

CAROL   Seem that all people do in this England is drink tea. I'll take a cup yes.

PHYLLIS   How you like the weather here?

CAROL   Jesus Mary and Joseph, don't mention it. It's as cold inside as it is out in the street.

PHYLLIS   It takes time to get accustomed. How you getting on with Peter?

CAROL   Girl, I don't know what to do. It's no that he's not good to me. He's a good man but–

PHYLLIS   What's the matter?

CAROL   He has this English girl that calls the house for him.

PHYLLIS   She's brazen. She doesn't know about you.

CAROL   Oh, I made her know.

PHYLLIS   What does he say?

CAROL   Well, I don't want to cause contention.

PHYLLIS   You don't want to cause contention, but wasn't it him who send for you to come?

CAROL   Yes.

PHYLLIS   And so?

CAROL   Well, he says that I must understand that he was lonely when he first come over and that it was this English girl who loaned him money when he couldn't find work.

Kettle whistling.

PHYLLIS   It's ready. Well, didn't he ask you to come?

CAROL   Yes, he said he wanted to get married.

PHYLLIS   Well then girl.

CAROL   I don't know what to do. *(Pause)* What you think?

PHYLLIS   I don't like to get between woman and man business.

CAROL   What would you do?

PHYLLIS   Well, I would put an end to that slackness. He would have to make a choice.

CAROL   But suppose he choose her?

PHYLLIS   *(Maternal tone, pours some rum in tea.)* Here's some lemon, drink it before it get cold. You must have more respect for yourself. If he sent for you then he must want you. You must sit down and have a serious talk with him.

CAROL   I was thinking of waiting.

PHYLLIS   Waiting for what?

CAROL   I was thinking that maybe if I was in a family way–

PHYLLIS   You're joking. Look girl, this is not back home. People could vanish here and you never see them again. You don't wait for that to happen, you clear the air now before it is too late. You have two feet, use them to stand up.

CAROL   I think you're right, you know. *(Sucks her teeth)* I'm going to talk to him tonight self. And if he says anything to me I'm going to give him tit for tat. As for that English girl she better give him a wide berth if she know what's good for she.

PHYLLIS   You better cook him a good dinner first.

CAROL   Oh yes, what shall I fix him?

PHYLLIS   Plenty of pilau *(They laugh)*

CAROL   And some dumplings and fry bakes.

PHYLLIS   And some ginger beer and a carrot cake to sweeten him.

CAROL   And when he can't move that's when I bust him in the arse with the news.

PHYLLIS   *(Singing)*
That's right the woman
is smarter
That's right the woman
is smarter
That's right.

They laugh.

Darkness.

SCENE V

The apartment two weeks later. Wallace returning from work.

PHYLLIS   That you, Wallace?

WALLACE   Who you think it is, the Prince of Wales?

PHYLLIS   You have a good day?

WALLACE   Any day that's over is a good day. *(Sits down heavily on chair and takes off shoes)*

PHYLLIS   You tired, put your feet up, rest. I'll get your dinner for you. You want to soak your feet?

WALLACE   I'm not so old yet.

PHYLLIS   I'm not saying you old. Soak your feet no, you'll feel better.

WALLACE   *(Pours drink of rum)* Well, this soon finish.

PHYLLIS   *(Brings a basin for him to soak feet)* Look, I bring you some water. I going put in some sea salt.

WALLACE   All right, then, if you insist.

PHYLLIS   I was talking with Doris today.

WALLACE   Doris?

PHYLLIS   You know Doris, at the market.

WALLACE   Doris at the market. Aye! this water is hot. *(Puts his feet to soak and starts to read papers)*

PHYLLIS   I think I'm going to join the sou-sou which she has going.

WALLACE   Sou-sou – what's that?

PHYLLIS   You know, every week you put in a pound and when your turn comes you get the whole thing. We could get up to a hundred pounds.

WALLACE   That's good.

PHYLLIS   Well, you know how these banks don't want to serve you if you coloured.

WALLACE   They don't mind as long as you putting money in. They just won't let you withdraw, that's all.

PHYLLIS   Don't you think the sou-sou is a good idea? I already give her a pound.

WALLACE   Fine, just don't say nothing if she tief the money.

PHYLLIS   You must trust somebody, Wallace.

WALLACE   I use to think so until I reach England.

PHYLLIS   I have a surprise for you.

WALLACE   Umhmm *(Still turning paper)*

PHYLLIS   *(Like a little girl)* Look, it come today.

WALLACE   What?

PHYLLIS   Well look no.

WALLACE   *(Looking over paper)* Oh, your sewing machine.

PHYLLIS   I send home for it.

WALLACE   Nice, now you can do my trousers.

PHYLLIS   I mean to do more than that. I think this is the answer to the problem.

WALLACE   Problem?

PHYLLIS   Money.

WALLACE   What you mean?

PHYLLIS   Now I can do some take home work.

WALLACE   *(Dropping paper)* What?

PHYLLIS   Look, Wallace, I don't mean to stay the rest of my life in one room.

WALLACE   I am not going to have you sewing.

PHYLLIS   Why not?

WALLACE   *(Picking up paper again)* We'll discuss it some other time. I'm hungry.

PHYLLIS   We'll discuss it now, Wallace.

PHYLLIS   Look, woman, don't make me have to box you, right?

PHYLLIS   I mean to send for the children.

WALLACE   Where are we going to put them?

PHYLLIS   That's why we have to move.

WALLACE   In time. We can't move yet.

PHYLLIS   That's why I want to do some seamstress work.

WALLACE   I'm not going to have my wife doing that.

PHYLLIS   Why not? The Jews do it.

WALLACE   Because we are not Jews, dammit.

PHYLLIS   For God's sake, man, we're living in one room on the top floor of a walk-up. Why must you put on airs. We're not back home. Back home we had two houses; here we have nothing.

WALLACE   We have pride.

PHYLLIS   I don't want pride, I want my two children.

WALLACE   Give it a year or two.

PHYLLIS   That's not good enough.

WALLACE   Well, it will have to do, you are not sewing people's clothes, and that's final.

PHYLLIS   Well, if you won't let me sew then I'll get a job doing what you're doing.

WALLACE   What you mean?

PHYLLIS   London Transport.

WALLACE   *(Jumping out of basin)* I'll kill you first.

PHYLLIS   Why not, just tell me why not, Wallace? I see many women doing it.

WALLACE   What would people say?

PHYLLIS   What people? They don't even know we're alive.

WALLACE   I won't have it. What did you come for? I never ask you to come. You came to make my life a misery.

PHYLLIS   Is who you fear for? For me or for yourself? You don't care if they say Wallace left his family and gone, but it frightens you to think that they might say Wallace have his wife taking in sewing or Wallace have his wife working London Transport.

WALLACE   Why you couldn't stay home in flipping Trinidad and leave me in peace?

PHYLLIS   Well, I'll tell you. Wherever you are is where I belong. I want the family, not just a piece of family. The whole family. And if I have to take some little kiss-me-arse job to do it, then I will. At least I will know why I'm working. Who have you been doing it for?

WALLACE   Who have I been doing it for? I've been doing it for –

PHYLLIS   For yourself. Just to punish yourself. It wasn't for me. If it was for me you would have stayed back home.

WALLACE   I did what I . . . what I had to do.

PHYLLIS   *(Watching Wallace walk out)* You don't have any shoes on, Wallace.

WALLACE   *(Slams door shut)* Dammit. I don't . . . I don't know where I'm going, Phyllis. Not any more. I use to know, but it's been a while now. You don't understand and I can't explain. It's different for a man. Hold me.

PHYLLIS   Hold me no. You think it's different for a woman.

WALLACE   Sometimes I feel like that chap Mittelholzer.

PHYLLIS   Edgar Mittelholzer? What come of him?

WALLACE   Set fire to himself last year.

PHYLLIS   Set fire to himself. Well, he must have been mad. He was doing so well back home.

WALLACE   This place can drive you mad. You lose things along the way, sometimes a tooth, sometimes family, occasionally you lose your mind.

PHYLLIS   Not me, it won't send me mad.

WALLACE   No, of course not. Not you, Phyllis. You could survive anywhere. I envy you. America, England, Canada. Anywhere. You will always survive.

PHYLLIS   Come eat.

WALLACE   I mean it, you're truly a survivor.

PHYLLIS   You make it sound like something sinful.

WALLACE   No, not at all.

PHYLLIS   Would you rather I was like some of these women who just sit back on they arse and expect their husband to do everything?

WALLACE   No, that's not you.

PHYLLIS   I think you would like that, you know. (Taunting) A wife that just settles for nothing, stay home and watch from the window, facing these factory gates.

WALLACE   So you want to work.

PHYLLIS   It's not for myself, it's for us, for the family. You must have something to hope for, otherwise –

WALLACE   You die.

PHYLLIS   Don't you miss the children, Wallace?

WALLACE   *(After a pause)* Do you think they still remember me? Carol does, I don't think Paul . . . well I don't know him very well, and yet he's the one who needs me most. Boys need their father, don't they?

PHYLLIS   Girls need their father too, Wallace. It's time now we come together.

WALLACE   Somehow I could talk more to the girl than the boy.

PHYLLIS   Well, you were always good with women.

WALLACE   You mamaguying me, eh?

PHYLLIS   I always thought maybe you had some English girl up here. Maybe you married her. I didn't quite know what to expect.

WALLACE   English girls were never my pleasure. I could never trust them in the kitchen. They don't know what salt fish is for.

PHYLLIS   *(Taunting)* Is not the kitchen I was thinking of.

WALLACE   Besides, they never like to bathe too much.

PHYLLIS   *(She laughs)* They smelling fresh, eh?

WALLACE   Well, you can't take a sea bath here, you know.

PHYLLIS   Barefoot boy. Come, let we eat no.

WALLACE   All right.

PHYLLIS   *(Gathering plates)* Lord, look at these plates. Soon as I start to work I'll fling all these into the bin. I don't understand how this man who used to eat off Wedgwood plates could live like this. Is like you become a monk or something.

WALLACE   Well, I did become one. I join the order of British
Trainsport ain't it. Pour me a small drop of that rum will
you. Careful there's not much left.

PHYLLIS   All right. Boy, it's getting cold you know. How people
could live here in the winter I don't know.

WALLACE   Those who can find work, work. Those who can't,
sleep through the winter if they can.

PHYLLIS   Here you are.

WALLACE   Thanks. Well you say you want to work. Go on then. I
won't stop you. I can't stop you anyway.

PHYLLIS   It's for the best, Wallace.

WALLACE   We'll see.

PHYLLIS   Well, we have no way to go but up. If they can own
houses, so can we.

WALLACE   You just come and your head is full of fire. Soon it
will be full of ice.

PHYLLIS   *(Kisses him)* Well, it's not as bad as when you first
came. There's more of we now.

WALLACE   Yes, there's more of we, so now it's worse. When we
first came it was just hate, they hated us. Now it's *fear* as
well as *hate*.

PHYLLIS   Is what we doing here at all? You call this life?

WALLACE   *(Slowly)* No, I never said this was life. I said this was
waiting. Waiting for life.

*Phyllis takes something out of a box. She calls to Wallace
teasingly. He looks up to see her holding a cricket bat.*

PHYLLIS   Psst! Hey Wallace, let's see some fast bowling no.

WALLACE   Where you find that?

PHYLLIS   Come on, fire one. I'm chasing boundary.

WALLACE   Girl, you too foolish.

PHYLLIS   Come on no, you 'fraid?

WALLACE   All right, watch this bowling line and length.

PHYLLIS   Wham. Six.

WALLACE   What! You'd be lucky.

PHYLLIS   *(Running about)* It's beyond the boundary, yes?

WALLACE   You never see me lick out your wicket. Is what
            happen to you.

PHYLLIS   Wallace, you glad I come?

WALLACE   Well . . .

PHYLLIS   You glad I come, yes or no?

WALLACE   It's all right.

PHYLLIS   I'll leave right now if you don't tell me. *(Tickling him)*

WALLACE   Stop tickling me. Yes, yes, I'm glad you reach. *(Pause)*
            I love you too bad, girl, but I don't know what to do with
            you.

PHYLLIS   Well, since you own up I'll feed you.

WALLACE   So you wasn't going to feed me.

PHYLLIS   If you didn't tell me you love me you would a fart
            tonight. Dog eat you supper.

WALLACE   *(Taking cricket bat)* Is not just for cricket they does use
            this you know. *(She runs laughing)*

            Music 'I'm Confessing'

WALLACE   And so, we work girl, and keep a shadow.
            And the only place we really live
            is in the secret sun of memory.
            You're right, is 'fraid I'm afraid,
            but maybe you'll show me how.

I never said this was life, girl.
I only said this was waiting.
Waiting on life.
And so we work girl, and keep a
shadow.

Curtain